Anonymus

Bill for amending Law relating to Local Government in Ireland

Anonymus

Bill for amending Law relating to Local Government in Ireland

ISBN/EAN: 9783741199851

Manufactured in Europe, USA, Canada, Australia, Japa

Cover: Foto ©Lupo / pixelio.de

Manufactured and distributed by brebook publishing software
(www.brebook.com)

Anonymus

Bill for amending Law relating to Local Government in Ireland

Local Government (Ireland) Bill.

ARRANGEMENT OF CLAUSES.

PART I.

COUNTY AND BARONIAL COUNCILS.

[Bill 174.]   a

PART II.

APPLICATION OF ACT TO COUNTIES OF CITIES AND TOWNS AND TO MUNICIPAL BOROUGHS.

PART III.

BOUNDARIES AND ADJUSTMENT OF PROPERTY AND LIABILITIES.

PART IV.

FINANCE.

Property Funds and Expenses of County Council.

PART V.

SUPPLEMENTAL.

Application of Acts.

PART VI.

TRANSITORY PROVISIONS.

First Election of County Councillors.

A

BILL

Amending the Law relating to Local Government in Ireland, A.D. 1892.
and for other purposes connected therewith.

BE it enacted by the Queen's most Excellent Majesty, by and
with the advice and consent of the Lords Spiritual and Tem-
poral, and Commons, in this present Parliament assembled, and by
the authority of the same, as follows:

5

PART I.

COUNTY AND BARONIAL COUNCILS.

1. A council (in this Act referred to as a county council or the
council of a county) shall be established in every administrative
county, and be entrusted with the management of the administra-
10 tive and financial business of that county, and shall consist of
a chairman and councillors (in this Act referred to as county
councillors).

2.—(1.) The county councillors shall be elected by the county
electors duly registered under this Act, and every person shall be
15 entitled to be so registered in every year who—

   (a) either is, or would, but for being a peer or a woman, be
   entitled to be, registered in that year, as a parliamentary elector
   for the county in respect of the occupation as owner or tenant
   of any property : and

20 (b) has, on or before the *first day of July* in that year, himself
   bonâ fide paid all county cess applotted on such property in
   the year ending on the preceding *first day of January*, or in
   the portion of that year during which he has been in
   occupation :

[Bill 174.]   A

*Part I.—
County
and Baronial
Councils.*

*Establish-
ment of
county
council.*

*Election of
councillors.*

(2.) Provided that—

(a) where an occupier is entitled to deduct the whole or part of the amount of the county cess from his rent, the Local Government Board, on the application of the immediate lessor, shall certify the average rate in the pound of county cess payable for the five years next before such application, and the occupier shall not be entitled to deduct from his rent more than would be deducted if the county cess amounted to such average rate; and 5

(b) if the immediate lessor is by law liable to pay the county cess, the occupier may, by written notice to the secretary to the county, claim to be solely liable to pay it, and thereupon he shall be, and be entered in the apportionment as, solely liable to pay the cess, but he shall be entitled, subject as above mentioned, to deduct the amount thereof from his rent. 10 · 15

(3.) The county councillors shall be elected for a term of three years, and shall then retire together, and their places shall be filled by a new election.

(4.) The Lord Lieutenant shall, within three months after the passing of this Act, determine the number of county councillors for each county, and whether a county is to be divided into electoral divisions, and if it is, the number and contents of those divisions, and the number of councillors to be elected in each division. 20

(5.) The councillors in each electoral division shall be elected by the county electors registered therein. 25

(6.) Every elector shall be entitled to a number of votes equal to the number of councillors to be elected, and may give all such votes to one candidate or distribute them among the candidates as he thinks fit.

(7.) The provisions of rule 20 in the First Schedule to the Ballot Act, 1872, as to voters making the declaration of inability to read shall not apply at any election under this Act. 30

Establish-
ment of
baronial
councils
and election
of council-
lors.

3.—(1.) A council (in this Act referred to as a baronial council or the council of a barony) shall be established in every administrative barony, and shall consist of a chairman and councillors (in this Act referred to as baronial councillors). 35

(2.) The foregoing provisions of this Act with respect to the constitution of county councils and election of councillors shall apply as if herein re-enacted with the substitution of barony for county, except that there shall be no electoral division of a barony, and the baronial councillors shall be elected by the county electors registered in the barony. 40

4.—(1.) For the purposes in that behalf in this Act mentioned there shall be a standing joint committee appointed by the grand jury and the council of every county, consisting of seven representatives appointed by each body, or such less number as the
5 two bodies may agree upon.

(2.) In addition to the representatives so appointed, the sheriff of the county, or during his absence from the county, sickness, or other inability to act, a person nominated for the purpose by the judge of assize at the first assizes in every year, shall be ex-officio a
10 member of the standing joint committee.

(3.) A resolution or act of the county council which involves any capital expenditure or capital liability, or the giving of any guarantee, or the undertaking to repair a road not previously repairable as a public road, shall, save as in this Act mentioned, be invalid without
15 the consent of the standing joint committee, and such consent may be given in whole or in part, and absolutely or conditionally.

5.—(1.) Any twenty cess payers of a county may apply to a judge of assize for leave to petition the High Court for the removal of the councillors of a county or baronial council, on the ground
20 of corruption, malversation, or oppression, or of persistent disobedience to the law, and the judge of assize, if of opinion, after hearing evidence, that there is a primâ facie case, may give such leave.

(2.) The petition shall be presented by the said cess payers within twenty-one days after leave is given, and shall be tried by the
25 judges on the rota for the trial of election petitions, and shall be presented and tried, and notice thereof served, and security for costs given, in like manner as nearly as may be as if the petition were an election petition.

(3.) At the conclusion of the trial the judges shall determine
30 whether the charges in the petition are or are not proved and—

(a) if they find proved a charge that a councillor knowingly and wilfully has committed an act of corruption, malversation, or oppression, or persistently disobeyed the law, they may disqualify him for seven years from holding office as a county
35 or baronial councillor; and

(b) if they find proved a charge of any act or default of the council which can be remedied, they may order the council to remedy that act or default within the time limited by the order; and

40 (c) if they find proved a charge that the council have knowingly pursued a course of corruption, malversation, oppression, or persistent disobedience to the law, they may order all the councillors to be removed;

A.D. 1892.
Part I.—
County and Baronial Councils.
Standing joint committee of grand jury and county council.

Removal of elected and substitution of appointed councillors.

and if any such order to remedy an act or default is not complied with by the council, the judge for the time being on the rota for the trial of election petitions may order all the councillors to be removed.

(4.) The judge shall in any case order by whom and in what proportions the costs are to be borne, whether by the council, by the councillors or any of them, or by the petitioners.

(5.) Upon an order of removal being made, the chairman and councillors of the council shall cease to hold office, and for such term, not exceeding *three years*, as is fixed by the order, such 10 persons, not less than five, qualified to be councillors of the council, as the Lord Lieutenant appoints (of whom one named by the Lord Lieutenant shall be chairman,) shall during his pleasure form the said council, and have the same authority and be in the same position as if elected councillors and chairman. 15

(6.) Within one month before the end of the said term, new councillors and a new chairman shall, on days fixed by the Lord Lieutenant, be elected, and if those days are not the ordinary days of election, they shall be elected as if they were the ordinary days of election, but the persons elected shall hold office for the same 20 time only as if they had been elected at the next preceding ordinary day of election. Until the day so fixed no councillors of such council shall be elected.

POWERS OF COUNTY AND BARONIAL COUNCILS.

Transfer of business of Grand Juries and Presentment Sessions. 25

Transfer to
county
council of
business of
grand jury
and county
at large pro-
sentment
sessions.

6.—(1.) Subject to the exceptions and provisions in this Act, there shall be transferred to the council of each county on and after the appointed day, the administrative business of the grand jury and of the presentment sessions of the county at large; and the expression administrative business includes all business in respect of 30 presentments for public works and moneys, and any fiscal concerns and fiscal business, and all business not excepted by this section; and anything authorised or required to be done by, to, or before a grand jury or the presentment sessions of a county at large in relation to such administrative business, shall be authorised or required to 35 be done by, to, or before the county council of the county without any fiat or other sanction of a judge of assize.

(2.) Nothing in this Act shall transfer to a county council or any committee or member thereof—

(a.) any business relating to bills of indictment or otherwise in 40 relation to criminal matters; or

A.D. 1899.

Part I.—
County
and Baronial
Councils.

6 & 7 Will. 4
c. 116.

(b.) any power to administer an oath; or

(a.) any business of the grand jury in relation to compensation
under section one hundred and six or section one hundred and
thirty-five of the Grand Jury Act, 1836, or any enactment of
5 that or any other Act touching such compensation, or applying
or amending either of those sections;

(3.) The application for such compensation shall be sent to the
grand jury through the secretary to the county, and not laid
before presentment sessions; and the time and procedure for making
10 the application shall be, so far as practicable, the same as heretofore, but may be adapted to this Act by the procedure rules under
this Act: Provided that,—

(a) where any jury is empannelled it shall be a special jury; and

(b) if the application is for compensation under the said section
15 one hundred and thirty-five the secretary shall send notice of
it to the council of the barony in which the offence giving rise
to it is alleged to have been committed, and that council may
appear as a party upon any hearing touching such application.

7. Subject to the exceptions and provisions in this Act,
20 there shall be transferred to the council of each barony on
and after the appointed day the business of the presentment
sessions of the barony, and anything authorised or required to be
done by, to, or before the presentment sessions of a barony shall
be authorised or required to be done by, to, or before the council
25 of the barony.

8.—(1.) Any applications (whether for works or for other matters
which but for that Act would have been made to the presentment
sessions of a barony) shall be made to the baronial council, and,
when approved by the council, be publicly notified and be sent
30 to and dealt with by the county council, within such time and
according to such procedure as, subject to the procedure rules,
may be determined by standing orders of the county council.

(2.) Every council (whether county or baronial) shall hold
quarterly meetings on such days and at such hours as (so far as
35 not fixed by this Act) are fixed by the county council. They shall
be so fixed that—

(a) a reasonable time shall elapse between every quarterly meeting of every baronial council in a county, and the next
quarterly meeting of the council of that county, and

40 (b) the county officers may be able to attend the meetings of all
the baronial councils.

Transfer to
baronial
council of
business of
baronial
presentment
sessions.

Time for
making of and
relations
between
county
council and
baronial
council.

A.D. 1872.

Part I.—
County
and Baronial
Councils.

6 & 7 Will. 4.
c. 116.

(3.) The Lord Lieutenant in Council may, within *six months after the passing of this Act*, make rules (in this Act referred to as procedure rules) regulating any such procedure under the Grand Jury Act, 1836, or any enactment applying or amending the same, as is affected by this Act, and any matter authorised by this 5 Act to be regulated by the procedure rules.

(4.) The procedure rules shall provide for the publicity of proceedings and resolutions of county and baronial councils, and for giving the like facilities for traverse and memorials as heretofore, but except so far as continued by the rules, or as applicable to any 10 business retained by the grand jury, the enactments relating to the procedure of grand juries as respects administrative business and of presentment sessions shall be repealed.

(5.) Subject to the provisions of this Act and of the enactments applied by this Act and of the procedure rules, every council may 15 make standing orders for the regulation of their proceedings and business, and for the purpose of aiding them in so doing, the Local Government Board may, if they think fit, frame and circulate model forms of standing orders.

(6.) Anything authorised or required to be done by, to, or 20 before a county or baronial council, may be done at such times and according to such procedure as, so far as not regulated by or in pursuance of this Act, may be determined by the said standing orders, but anything so required to be done shall be done at the time necessary for giving effect to such requirement. 25

9.—(1.) Subject as in this section mentioned every person shall be entitled to the like traverse as heretofore.

(2.) The traverse, if entered more than one month before the next assizes for the county, may be entered in the High Court, and there tried; but may, if rules of the High Court so provide or the 30 Court so order, be remitted for trial to a judge of assize, or (whatever may be the amount involved) to the Civil Bill Court.

(3.) The traverse shall be tried in like manner as heretofore, save that it shall, if not tried in the Civil Bill Court, be tried by a special jury; and there shall be the same appeal from any decision 35
of the Civil Bill Court as is conferred by the County Court Amendment (Ireland) Act, 1882, and the Acts amending the same.

(4.) Subject as in this section mentioned all persons shall be entitled to the like power as heretofore of presenting a memorial under section eighteen or section sixty-four of the Grand Jury Act, 40 1836, and any other enactments relating to the like memorial, and such memorial shall be dealt with in like manner as heretofore, save that where a jury is empannelled it shall be a special jury.

(5.) Rules of the High Court shall be made for carrying into effect this section and adapting to this Act the procedure relating
5 to traverses and the said memorials.

A.D. 1892.

Part I.—
County
and Baronial
Councils.

Transfer of Miscellaneous Powers.

10. There shall be transferred to the council of each county on and after the appointed day the business of any board of guardians in any area in the county in relation to the execution as local
10 authority of the Contagious Diseases (Animals) Acts, 1878 to 1890, and the Destructive Insects Act, 1877.

Transfer to
county
council of
certain diseases
powers.
41 & 42 Vict.
c. 74.
33 & 34 Vict.
c. 14.

11. There shall be transferred to the council of each county on and after the appointed day, the business of any justices as to the repair of sudden damage to roads, whether under section forty-nine
15 of the Grand Jury Act, 1836, or under the Roads Act, 1807, or otherwise, but without any limitation as to the number of orders which may be made.

Transfer
of powers
as to sudden
damage
to roads.
80 & 81 Vict.
c. 112.

12.—(1.) A county council may resolve to adopt this section in their county and cause such resolution to be published at least
20 twice in two newspapers circulating generally in the county, and if the resolution is confirmed by a resolution of the council at a meeting held not less than one month after the first of such publications, the adoption shall, at the end of three months after such confirming resolution, or at any later date thereby fixed,
25 take effect.

Power of
county
council to
take over
powers of
rural
sanitary
authorities.

(2.) Thereupon there shall be transferred to the council of the county the business of every board of guardians in any area in the county touching the execution as rural sanitary authority of the Sanitary Acts, and in this Act the expression " Sanitary
30 Acts" means the Public Health (Ireland) Act, 1878, the Housing of the Working Classes Act, 1890, the Labourers (Ireland) Acts, 1883 to 1886, and the Factory and Workshop Act, 1891, and the Acts amending any of the said Acts, and any other Act conferring powers and duties on rural sanitary authorities as such.

41 & 42 Vict.
c. 52.
53 & 54 Vict.
c. 70.
46 & 47 Vict.
c. 60.
49 & 19 Vict.
c. 77.
49 & 50 Vict.
c. 59.
54 & 55 Vict.
c. 75.

35 (3.) The county council shall, for the administration of the business so transferred, divide their county into such districts (in this Act called sanitary districts), as with the approval of the Local Government Board they think suitable (so that each townland be wholly included in one district), and shall delegate the said

administration in each sanitary district to a committee (in this
Act called a sanitary committee) appointed from time to time
and consisting of such county councillors and such councillors
of the baronies comprised wholly or partly in the district as appear
to the county council to represent the cesspayers of the district.   5

(4.) The sanitary committee shall have within the sanitary district all the powers, duties, and liabilities of the rural sanitary
authority under the Sanitary Acts, subject nevertheless to the
provisions of this Act and subject as follows :—

(a) a sanitary committee shall have no power in relation to 10
officers, and no power of raising money by rate, cess, or loan ;

(b) the power of adopting any Act or enactment shall be
exercised by the county council either for their county or for
any sanitary district :

(c) the county council shall make general regulations for the 15
government of the sanitary committee, to which the committee
shall conform ;

(d) any five cesspayers in the barony may appeal to the county
council from any act or order of the sanitary committee
other than any proceedings for the removal of a nuisance, 20
and the county council may confirm, vary, or rescind such act
or order, and pending appeal, such act or order shall be stayed ;

(e) A medical officer or sanitary inspector of the county may
appeal to the county council in relation to any act or order
of the sanitary committee, and thereupon the council may 25
make an order under the Sanitary Acts.

(5.) The consent of the standing joint committee shall not be
required to any expenditure for the purposes of the Sanitary Acts
which is defrayed out of special expenses.

(6.) The power of appointing officers under the Sanitary Acts is 30
hereby varied, so that the county council may appoint officers
either for the whole county, or for any part thereof, and may
assign the area within which any such officer is to exercise
his office. The officers so appointed shall hold their office by the
like tenure and have, as nearly as may be, within the area assigned 35
the same powers and duties as the officers of the sanitary
authority have within the district of that authority.

(7.) The expenses of the execution of the Sanitary Acts in any
sanitary district shall be levied off the district, or the proper
contributory place in the district.   40

(8.) The county council may delegate to a sanitary committee the business respecting the repair of sudden damage to roads.

(9.) If the county council are of opinion that the sanitary committee have made default in performing any duty, the council shall take the necessary steps to secure the performance of that duty, and for that purpose may exercise all the powers of the sanitary authority.

(10.) If it appears to the Lord Lieutenant that the councils of not less than three-fourths in number of all the counties in Ireland have adopted this section, he may, by Order in Council, direct, that the section shall have effect in the remaining counties as if adopted, and make such provisions as seem necessary or proper for that purpose, and the order shall have the same effect in each of those counties as a duly confirmed resolution of the council of that county.

13.—(1.) On and after the appointed day, a county council shall have power, in addition to any other authority (if any), to enforce the Rivers Pollution Prevention Act, 1876 (subject to the restrictions in that Act contained), in relation to so much of any stream as is situate within or passes through or by any part of their county, and for that purpose they shall have the same powers and duties as if they were a sanitary or other authority having power to enforce that Act, and the county were their district.

(2.) A county council may contribute towards the costs of any prosecution under the said Act instituted by any other county council or any sanitary authority.

(3.) The Local Government Board by Provisional Order made on the application of the council of any county concerned, may constitute a joint committee or other body representing all the counties through or by which a river, or any specified portion of a river, or any tributary thereof, passes, and may confer on such committee or body all or any of the powers of a sanitary authority under the said Act; and the Order may contain such provisions respecting the constitution and proceedings of the said committee or body as may seem proper, and may provide for the payment of the expenses of such committee or body by the counties represented by it, and for the audit of the accounts of such committee or body and their officers.

14. Where it appears to the Local Government Board that any business under a local Act of any grand jury, presentment sessions, board of guardians, or other local authority is similar in character to that transferred to county or baronial councils by this

[174.]   B

A.D. 1892.

Part I.
County and Baronial Councils.

Power of county council to enforce provisions of 39 & 40 Vict. c. 75.

Power to transfer powers under local Acts.

Part I.
County
and
Boroinial
Councils.

Act, or relates to property so transferred, the Board may, make a Provisional Order for transferring such business to a council.

New Powers.

Appointment
of governors
of lunatic
asylums.

15.—(1.) On and after the appointed day the council of each county may appoint to be governors or directors of the district 5 lunatic asylum for the county or district comprising the county, such number of persons as the Lord Lieutenant authorises, and the persons so appointed shall hold office during the term of office of the council that appointed them.

(2.) Nothing in this section shall limit the existing power of the 10 Lord Lieutenant to appoint governors or directors of an asylum, save that the number appointed by him shall not exceed the aggregate number of governors or directors of that asylum authorised to be appointed by county councils.

Appoint-
ment of
governors
of public
Infirmaries
and hospitals.

16. Every county council may appoint annually five persons 15 to be governors of any infirmary or hospital in their county to which contribution has been or is in the course of being made out of the county cess, and those governors shall be members of the body corporate of the infirmary or hospital, and have all the powers of fully qualified governors. 20

Appointment
of coroners
by county
council.

17.—(1.) After the appointed day a coroner for a county shall not be elected by the parliamentary electors of the county or any district therein, and on a vacancy in the office of a coroner for a county, who is elected to that office in pursuance of a writ de coronatore eligendo, a like writ for the election of a successor 25 shall be directed to the council of the county instead of to the sheriff, and the council shall thereupon appoint a qualified person, not being a county or baronial councillor, to the office, and if the county is divided into coroners districts, assign him a district.

(2.) The enactments relating to the division of a county, riding, 30 or division into coroners districts shall have effect as if the county council were substituted for the justices in special sessions.

See 23 & 31
Vict. c. 116.
50 & 51 Vict.
c. 71, s. 8.

(3.) The Lord Chancellor may, if he thinks fit, remove any coroner from his office for inability or misbehaviour in the discharge of his duty. Nothing in this section shall alter the jurisdiction 35 of the Lord Chancellor or the High Court or a judge of assize, in relation to the removal of a coroner otherwise than in manner provided by this Act.

(4.) All writs for the election or removal of a coroner shall be altered so as to give effect to this section. 40

A.D. 1892.

Part I.
County
and
Baronial
Councils.

(5.) A person who is coroner for a county shall not be qualified to be elected a county or baronial councillor in that county.

18.—(1.) The council of each county shall, upon the report of the county surveyor, determine what roads in the county shall be 5 main roads, and *one half* of the expenses of the maintenance or improvement of any main road shall be levied off the county at large and the other half off the baronies in which the road is situate.

(2.) After *six months* from the appointed day no sum shall be levied off the county at large in respect of any road not deter-10 mined under this section to be a main road.

(3.) Any baronial council, if aggrieved by any determination under this section or by the refusal or failure of the council to determine any road to be a main road, may appeal to the Local Government Board, and a determination of the county council reversed by 15 that Board shall be of no effect, and an order of that Board shall operate as a determination by the council.

19. Where, on the representation of the council of any barony, it appears to the county council that the preservation of any wood or plantation would be advantageous to the barony, the county council 20 may at the cost of the barony acquire by agreement such wood or plantation, and manage and preserve it.

20. The council of a county shall have the same powers of opposing bills in Parliament and of prosecuting and defending legal proceedings necessary for the promotion or protection of the 25 interests of the inhabitants of the county, as are conferred on the governing body in any district by the Borough Funds (Ireland) Act, 1888; and that Act shall extend to a county council as if they were a "governing body" and the administrative county were their district: except that—

30 (a.) the consent of the standing joint committee shall be required to any action of the county council under the said Act;

(b.) no consent of owners or ratepayers shall be required; and

(c.) this section shall not empower a county council to promote any Bill in Parliament, or to incur or defray any expenses in 35 relation thereto.

21.—(1.) The Local Government Board may, with the consent of the board or body affected, make Provisional Orders for transferring to county councils any business arising in the county under any statute, of any drainage board, or other public body, corporate 40 or unincorporate (not being town commissioners, or an urban or rural sanitary authority, or a board of guardians); and each Order

[174.] B 2

A.D. 1802.
Part I.
County
and
Baronial
Councils.

shall make such exceptions and modifications as appear to be expedient, and also such provisions as appear necessary or proper for carrying into effect the transfer.

(2.) Any such business if arising within two or more counties, may be transferred to the councils of those counties jointly, and be administered by a joint committee.

Miscellaneous.

General provisions as to powers transferred to councils.

22. A county or baronial council shall, as respects the business by this Act transferred to them from any authority, be subject to the provisions and limitations in this Act specified, but, save as aforesaid, shall have all the powers, duties, and liabilities of the authority in respect of the business transferred.

Summary proceedings for determination of questions as to transfer of powers.

23. If any question arises, or is about to arise, as to whether any business, power, duty, or liability is or is not transferred to any county or baronial council under this Act, or as to the extent or time or mode of exercise or performance, of any power or duty transferred, or as to the right of any authority or person affected by such transfer, or by the provisions of this Act relating thereto, or as to whether the consent of the standing joint committee is or is not required, that question, without prejudice to any other mode of trying it, may, on the application of any county or baronial council, standing joint committee, grand jury, board of guardians, or persons concerned, be submitted for decision to the High Court in such summary manner as, subject to rules of court, may be directed by the court; and the court, after hearing such parties and taking such evidence (if any) as it thinks just, shall decide the question; and every such decision shall be subject to appeal.

PART II.

APPLICATION OF ACT TO COUNTIES OF CITIES AND TOWNS AND TO MUNICIPAL BOROUGHS.

A.D. 1891.

Part II.— Application of Act to Towns.

Application of Act to existing counties of cities and towns.

24.—(1.) Where a county of a city or town is co-extensive with a municipal borough this Act shall apply thereto in like manner as to a county at large, subject as follows :—

(a) The council of the borough shall be the county council, but, except in Dublin, the burgesses electing the council shall have, in substitution for their existing qualification, the like qualification as is provided by this Act respecting county electors, with the substitution for "county cess," of every rate assessed by the council of the borough, and, where the municipal borough is comprised in a parliamentary borough, with the substitution of "parliamentary borough" for "county";

(b) There shall be no standing joint committee or baronial council, and the council of the borough shall have the powers and duties of the baronial council;

(c) The provisions of Part One respecting—

(i.) the removal of elected and the substitution of appointed councillors; or

(ii.) the transfer of the business of rural sanitary authorities; or

(iii.) the appointment of coroner: or

(iv.) main roads; or

(v.) the application of the Borough Funds (Ireland) Act, 1888;

shall not apply;

(d) References to the fiat or sanction of the judge of assize shall be construed to include the fiat or sanction of the recorder, and references to the secretary to the county shall be construed to refer to the town clerk;

(e) Part Four, Part Five, and Part Six, except so far as relates to the powers of the Local Government Board and Privy Council, and the definitions of this Act, shall not apply save as therein expressly provided;

(f) The county of a city or town shall be a county borough within this Act.

(2.) Where a county of a town is not co-extensive with a municipal borough, a charter shall be issued under the Municipal Corporations (Ireland) Acts, incorporating the inhabitants of the county of the town, and a council shall be elected accordingly; and the fore-

going provisions of this section shall apply to the county of the
town and to such council.

(3.) There shall be transferred to such last-mentioned council on
and after the appointed day the business as respects any area in the
borough of the commissioners under any local Act (who shall there-   5
upon cease to hold office), but the councillors elected for any ward
situate wholly outside the said area shall not vote or act in relation
to that business: Provided that where such business relates to a
harbour, it shall not be transferred to the council, and the Local
Government Board by an order under Part Three of this Act shall 10
provide for the continuance of the said commissioners for the transaction of the harbour business, and for the exercise and discharge of
the powers, duties, and liabilities connected therewith.

(4.) The coroner of the county of the town of Galway shall be
appointed by the council as in the case of any other municipal 15
borough.

25.—(1.) Each municipal borough which is not a county of a
city or town shall, on and after the appointed day, be for the
purposes of this Act an administrative county of itself, and a
county borough within this Act, provided that—   20

(a.) for all other purposes the borough shall continue to be part
of the same county at large as heretofore ; and

(b.) an equitable adjustment of the financial relations of the
borough and the said county, shall, if not made by any Act
passed during the present session, be made by agreement within 25
twelve months after the appointed day between the councils
concerned, and until any such adjustment takes effect the
financial relations shall continue as heretofore ;

(2.) The foregoing provisions of this Part of this Act shall apply
to a county borough constituted by this section in like manner as 30
if it were a county of a city or town, and as if the grand jury
and presentment sessions of the county at large and the presentment sessions of the barony had, so far as regards the area within
the borough, been a grand jury and presentment sessions of the
county borough ;   35

(3.) Provided that in Belfast the burgesses shall continue to have
their existing qualification.

26.—(1.) Where the town commissioners of a town are the road
authority, that town shall be separated from any barony of which

heretofore the town or any part of the town has formed part, but
shall continue liable as heretofore to county cess levied off the
county at large; and without prejudice to the existing powers of
the town commissioners, the enactments of this Act, and any other
5 Act relating to baronies, shall apply to such town, as if it were a
separate barony, and as if the commissioners of such town, who
shall be elected under the general or local Acts relating to the
town, were the council of that barony.

(2.) Any determination of the county council or order of the
10 Local Government Board in respect of main roads shall take
into account any privileges or exemptions of any such town under
any Act or provisional order confirmed by an Act.

(3.) An equitable adjustment of the financial relations of the town
and barony shall be made by agreement within *twelve months* after
15 the appointed day between the council and town commissioners
concerned, and until any such adjustment takes effect, the financial
relations shall continue as heretofore, and any such adjustment shall
take into account the privileges or exemptions above mentioned.

27.—(1.) Where an existing barony is partly within and partly
20 without a county borough or a town separated from the barony by
this Act the remainder of the barony which is without the borough
or town shall be a barony of itself ; save that if it contains a population of less than five thousand, the Local Government Board shall
by order either unite it to an adjoining barony, or divide it and
25 unite different parts of it to adjoining baronies, and an equitable
adjustment of financial relations shall be made by agreement,
within twelve months after the appointed day, between the councils
and town commissioners concerned.

(2.) Any adjustment under this part of this Act may in
30 default of agreement within the said *twelve* months be made by
order of the Local Government Board, but any council or commissioners, if dissatisfied with the order, may appeal to the Privy
Council, and the adjustment shall be made by an Order in Council
made in accordance with the advice given by the Privy Council
35 after hearing such appeal.

(3.) Any adjustment under this part of this Act may be altered
at any time after *five years* from the date thereof either by agreement,
or in default of agreement, by the Local Government Board, or by
the Privy Council on appeal.

A.D. 1898.

*Part II.—
Application
of Act to
Towns.*

Supple-
mental as to
barony
divided by
borough or
town and as to
adjustment
of financial
relations.

A.D. 1892.

Part III.—
Boundaries
and Adjust-
ment of
Property
and
Liabilities.
Boundary of
county.

PART III.

BOUNDARIES AND ADJUSTMENT OF PROPERTY AND LIABILITIES.

28.—(L) The first council elected under this Act for an administrative county not a county borough shall be elected for the county at large for which a grand jury has been accustomed to be 5 summoned, and, where a grand jury has been accustomed to be summoned for a riding, shall be elected for that riding : except that—

(a) there shall be excluded the county boroughs ; and

(b) any town separated by this Act from a barony and situate 10 partly in two counties, shall form part of that county which contains the largest portion of the population of the town.

(2.) The county for the first election shall, subject to alteration as in this Act mentioned, continue to be, for all the purposes of this Act, an administrative county and be the county of the county 15 council.

(3.) Any difference as to the county which contains the largest portion of the population of any town shall be referred to the Local Government Board, whose decision shall be final.

29.—(1.) The first council elected under this Act for an 20 administrative barony shall be elected for the barony, for which at the assizes next before the *passing of this Act* presentment sessions were appointed to be held ; except that

(a) there shall be excluded a borough constituted a county borough and a town separated by this Act from the barony ; 25 and

(b) there shall be added to it any part of a barony united to it under this Act.

(2.) The barony for the first election shall, subject to alteration as in this Act mentioned, continue to be, for all the purposes of 30 this Act, an administrative barony and be the barony of the baronial council.

30.—(1.) Whenever it is represented by the council of any county, barony, or municipal borough or by any town commissioners to the Local Government Board— 35

(a) that the alteration of the boundary of any county, barony, or town is desirable ; or

(b) that the union, for all or any of the purposes of this Act, of a county borough with a county at large is desirable; or

(c) that, for all or any of the purposes of this Act, the union of any counties, baronies, or towns, or the division of any county or barony is desirable; or

(d) that the alteration or union of the electoral divisions of a county, or wards of a municipal borough, or the division of a county into electoral divisions, or the alteration of the number of councillors of a county, electoral division, or barony is desirable; or

(e) that the alteration of any area of local government partly situate in their county or barony is desirable;

the Board shall, unless for special reasons they think that the representation ought not to be entertained, cause to be made a local inquiry, and may make an order for the proposal contained in such representation, or for such other proposal as they deem expedient, or may refuse the order.

(2.) If the order alters the boundary of a county or town, or unites a county borough to a county at large, or unites any counties or baronies or divides any county or barony, or alters the electoral divisions of a county, or divides a county into electoral divisions, it shall be only a provisional order.

(3.) An order under this section may, as consequential thereon, do all or any of the following things—increase or decrease the number of the wards in the borough, alter the boundaries of such wards, the apportionment of the number of councillors among the wards, and the total number of councillors, and in the latter case, proportionately alter the number of aldermen.

(4.) Any existing power to make any union, division, or alteration which can be made under this section shall cease.

31.—(1.) An order under this Act may make such administrative and judicial arrangements incidental to or consequential on any alteration of boundaries, authorities, or other matters, made by the order, as may seem expedient.

(2.) A place which is part of an administrative county for the purposes of this Act shall, subject as in this Act mentioned, form

Margin notes:

A.D. 1892.

Part III.—
Boundaries
and Adjustment of
Property
and
Liabilities.

Supplemental provisions as to alteration of areas.

A.D. 1888.

Part III.—
Boundaries
and Adjust-
ment of
Property
and
Liabilities.

part of that county for all purposes, whether sheriff, lieutenant, custos rotulorum, justices, militia, coroner or other ; Provided that—

(a) If a county borough is, at the *passing of this Act*, a part of any county for any of the above purposes, nothing in this Act   5
shall prevent the same from continuing to be part of that county for that purpose; and

(b) this enactment shall not affect parliamentary elections nor the right to vote at such elections.

(3.) For the purpose of parliamentary elections, and of the   10
registration of parliamentary electors, the sheriff, and clerk of the peace of the county in which any place is comprised at the *passing of this Act* for such purpose shall, save as otherwise provided by the order, or by or in pursuance of this Act, continue to have the same powers, duties, and liabilities as if no alteration of boundary   15
had taken place, and the expenses connected therewith shall form the subject of adjustment under this Act.

(4.) Any order made in pursuance of this Act may, so far as seems necessary or proper for the purposes of the order, provide for all or any of the following matters, that is to say,—   20

(a) may provide for the abolition, restriction, or establishment, or extension of the jurisdiction of, any local authority in or over any part of the area affected by the order, and for the adjustment or alteration of the boundaries of such area, and for the constitution of the local authorities therein, and may   25
deal with the powers and duties of any council, commissioners, local authorities, quarter or general sessions, justices of the peace, coroners, sheriff, lieutenant, custos rotulorum, clerk of the peace, and other officer therein, and with the costs of any such council, commissioners, authorities, sessions, persons, or   30
officers as aforesaid, and may determine the status of any such area as a component part of any larger area, and provide for the election of representatives in such area, and may extend to any altered area the provisions of any local Act which were previously in force in a portion of the area ; and   35

(b) may make temporary provision for meeting the debts and liabilities of the various authorities affected by the order, for the management of their property, and for regulating the duties, position, and remuneration of officers affected by

A.D. 1898.

Part III.—
Boundaries
and Adjust-
ment of
Property
and
Liabilities.

the order, and applying to them the provisions of this Act
as to existing officers ; and

  (c) may provide for the transfer of any writs, process, records,
and documents relating to or to be executed in any part of
the area affected by the order, and for determining questions
arising from such transfer ; and

  (d) may provide for all matters which appear necessary or proper
for bringing into operation and giving full effect to the order;
and

  (e) may adjust any property, debts, and liabilities affected by the
order.

(5.) Where this Act alters the boundaries of a county or abolishes
or affects any town or municipal commissioners, an order for any of
the above-mentioned matters may, if it appears desirable, be made
by the Local Government Board, but the order, if petitioned
against by any council, grand jury, sessions, commissioners, or local
authority affected thereby, within *three* months after the prescribed
notice of it is given, shall, unless the petition is withdrawn, be only
a provisional order.

(6.) An order for amending any previous order under this Act
may be made by the same authority and after the same procedure
as the previous order.

(7.) An order under this Act which requires confirmation by
Parliament, either in every case or if it is petitioned against, may
amend any local Act.

32.—(1.) Any councils, commissioners, boards of guardians, and
other authorities affected by this Act, or by any order or thing made
or done under this Act, may make agreements for the purpose
of adjusting any property, income, debts, liabilities, and expenses,
so far as thus affected, of the parties to the agreement.

(2.) Any adjustment of financial relations under this Act may
provide for the transfer or retention of any property, debts, and
liabilities, with or without any conditions, and for the joint use of
any property, and for the transfer of any duties, and for
payment by either party to the adjustment in respect of property,
debts, duties, and liabilities so transferred or retained, or in respect
of such joint use, and in respect of the salary, remuneration,
superannuation allowance, or compensation payable to any officer
or person, and that either by way of a capital sum or of a
terminable annuity for a period not exceeding that allowed by
the Local Government Board.

A.D. 1892.

Part III.—
Boundaries
and Adjust-
ment of
Property
and
Liabilities.
8 & 9 Vic.
c. 18.

(8.) In default of an agreement any adjustment under this Act may be made by an arbitrator appointed by the parties, or, in case of difference as to the appointment, by the Local Government Board.

(4.) An arbitrator appointed under this Act shall be an arbi- 5
trator within the meaning of the Lands Clauses Acts, and the
provisions of those Acts with respect to an arbitration shall
apply accordingly; and further, the arbitrator may state a special
case, and, notwithstanding anything in the said Acts, shall determine the amount of the costs, and may disallow as costs in the 10
arbitration the expenses of any witness whom he considers to have
been called unnecessarily, and any other expenses which he
considers to have been incurred unnecessarily.

(5.) A sum payable for the purpose of an adjustment under this
Act may be paid out of the county or borough fund or out of such 15
special fund as the council, with the approval of the Local Government Board, may direct, and if it is a capital sum, its payment
shall be a purpose for which a council or town commissioners may
borrow under the enactments relating to their borrowing, and such
sum may be borrowed on the security of all or any of their funds, 20
rates, and revenues, and either by the creation of stock or in any
other authorised manner, and such sum may be borrowed without
the consent of the Local Government Board or any other authority,
so that it be repaid within the period sanctioned by the Board
by such method as is mentioned in Part Four of this Act, or is 25
directed by or in pursuance of the said enactments relating to
borrowing.

(6.) A capital sum paid to any council or commissioners for
any adjustment, shall be treated as capital, and applied, with the
sanction of the Local Government Board, either for repaying debt or 30
for any other purpose for which capital money may be applied.

PART IV.

FINANCE.

Property Funds and Expenses of County Council.

A.D. 1892.

Part IV.—
Finance.

Transfer of
county pro-
perty and
liabilities.

33.—(1.) On and after the appointed day all the property of the county, or held by any commissioners or person on behalf of the grand jury or for any public uses and purposes of a county, shall pass to and vest in and be held in trust for the council of the county, subject to all debts and liabilities affecting it, and shall be held by the county council for the same estate, interest, and purposes, and subject to the same covenants, conditions, and restrictions, for and subject to which that property is or would have been held if this Act had not passed, so far as those purposes are not modified by this Act;

Provided that the grand jury of any county may retain any pictures, plate, chattels, or property on the ground that the same have been presented to them, or purchased out of their own funds, or otherwise belong to them, and are not held for public purposes of the county.

(2.) On and after the appointed day all debts and liabilities incurred for county purposes shall become debts and liabilities of the county council, and shall, subject to the provisions of this Act, be defrayed by them out of the like property and funds out of which they would have been defrayed if this Act had not passed.

(3.) The foregoing provisions shall apply as respects the property, debts, and liabilities of any authority whose business is transferred by this Act to the county council so far as the property is held for, and the debts and liabilities were incurred on account of, the business transferred; and where the transfer of the business takes effect only upon a resolution of the county council or Order in Council, the appointed day shall be deemed to be the date at which such transfer takes effect.

(4.) Any difference arising as to whether any property is, or should be, by virtue of this section, transferred to the council of a county, shall be decided finally by the Local Government Board.

(5.) A council of a county shall have full power to manage, alter, and enlarge, and, with the consent of the Local Government Board, to alienate, lease, and dispose of any land or buildings transferred by this section, or otherwise vested in or held in trust for the council, but a county council shall provide such accommodation and rooms, and such furniture, books, and other things as may be determined by the standing joint committee to be necessary or proper for the due transaction of the business of such committee, and of the grand jury, and for the due transaction of the business and convenient keeping of the records and documents of the quarter sessions and justices of the peace.

(d.) This section shall apply to the counties of cities and towns 5 which are constituted county boroughs, but with the substitution of the council for the standing joint committee.

34.—(1.) All receipts of the county council from whatever source, whether for general or special purposes, shall be carried to the county fund, and all payments for general or special purposes 10 shall be made in the first instance out of that fund.

(2.) In this Act the expression "general purposes" means all purposes declared by this or any other Act to be general purposes, and all purposes for which the county council are for the time being authorised by law to levy county cess off the whole 15 county; and the expression "general expenses account" means the account of the county fund to which the cess levied off the whole county is carried; and any expenses incurred for a general purpose shall be general expenses, and expenses incurred by the county council in the execution of their duties which are not 20 by law made special expenses shall be general expenses.

(3.) In this Act the expression "special purposes" means any purposes for which the county council are authorised to levy a cess off any barony, sanitary district, townland, or other limited area in the county only; and the expression "special account" means any 25 account of the county fund to which county cess levied for special purposes is carried, and special expenses shall include any expenses incurred for a special purpose.

(4.) If the moneys standing to the general expenses account of the county fund are insufficient to meet the general expenses, the 30 county council shall apply on, and levy off, the whole county county cess to meet the deficiency.

(5.) If the moneys standing to any special account of the county fund are insufficient to meet the special expenses chargeable to that account the county council shall apply on and levy 35 off the barony, sanitary district, townland, or other area in the county liable for those expenses county cess to meet the deficiency.

(6.) The applotment of county cess shall include all items to be levied whether for general or special expenses.

(7.) The county council shall keep such accounts as will 40 prevent the whole county from being charged with expenditure properly payable by a part only of the county, and will prevent a part only of the county from being charged with

expenditure properly payable by the whole or a different part of
the county, and will prevent any sums by law specifically applicable to any particular purpose from being applied to any other
purpose.

5 (8.) In determining the amount of expenditure for any purpose,
a proper proportion of the expenses of the county officers and buildings may be added to the expenditure directly expended for
that purpose.

35.—(1.) All payments to and out of the county fund shall be
10 made to and by the county treasurer, and all payments out of the
fund shall, unless made in pursuance of the specific requirement of
an Act of Parliament or of an order of a judge of assize or com-
petent court, be made in pursuance of an order of the council signed
by three members of the finance committee present at the meeting
15 of the council and countersigned by the secretary to the county
or by a deputy authorised by the council, and the same order
may include several payments, and shall be sent to the county
treasurer.

(2.) No money shall be paid by the treasurer to any person
20 except on a draft payable to him or his order, and having endorsed
thereon a receipt expressing the purpose for which the amount of
the draft is paid, and such draft shall be signed by some member
of the finance committee and by the secretary to the county or
by a deputy authorised by the council.

25 36.—(1.) The county council, with the consent of the standing
joint committee and the Local Government Board, may borrow, on
the security of the county fund and any revenues of the council, or
either of such fund or revenues, or any part of the revenues, the
sums required for the following purposes, or any of them, that is
30 to say;

(a.) for consolidating the debts of the county; and

(b.) for purchasing any land or building any building, which the
council are authorised by any Act to purchase or build; and

(c.) for any permanent work or other thing which the county
35 council are authorised to execute or do, and the cost of which
ought in the opinion of the Local Government Board to be
spread over a term of years; and

(d.) for any purpose in relation to any business transferred to the
county council for which at the *passing of this Act* a loan is
40 authorised to be raised;

but neither the transfer of powers by this Act nor anything else
in this Act shall confer on the county council any power to

borrow without the consent above mentioned, and the Local Government Board, before giving their consent, shall take into consideration any representation made by any payer of, or any owner of property liable to, the county cess.

(2.) Provided that where the total debt of the county council, after deducting the amount of any sinking fund, exceeds, or if the proposed loan is raised will exceed, *one-tenth* of the rateable value of the county, the loan shall not be borrowed, except in pursuance of a provisional order made by the Local Government Board.

(3.) A loan under this section shall be repaid within such period, not exceeding *thirty* years, as the county council, with the said consent, determine in each case, and either by equal yearly or half-yearly instalments of principal, or of principal and interest combined, or by means of a sinking fund set apart, invested, and applied in accordance with the stock regulations in this section mentioned.

(4.) Where a loan is raised for any special purpose, the council shall take care that the sums payable by them in respect of the loan are charged to the special account to which the expenditure for that purpose is chargeable.

(5.) The county council where authorised to borrow any money may borrow it either as one loan or several loans by stock issued in accordance with the stock regulations under section fifty-two of the Public Health Acts Amendment Act, 1890, which section is hereby incorporated with this Act and made applicable to counties, or if special reasons exist for so borrowing, by mortgage, and sections two hundred and forty to two hundred and forty-three of the Public Health (Ireland) Act, 1878, shall apply to such mortgage;

(6.) Provided that a county council who have borrowed by means of stock shall not borrow by way of mortgage except for a period not exceeding *five years*.

37. After the appointed day the Local Government Board shall exercise, as regards any municipal borough, the powers and duties under the Municipal Corporations (Ireland) Acts relating to borrowing, and to the purchase, alienation, sale, lease, or other disposition of land, and those provisions shall, as respects transactions commenced after the appointed day, be construed as if "Local Government Board" were throughout substituted for "Treasury."

38.—(1.) The accounts of the receipts and expenditure of county councils shall be made up to the end of each local financial year as defined by this Act, and be in the prescribed form.

(2.) The accounts of every county council shall be audited by such auditor of poor law unions as may be appointed by the Local

A.D. 1892.
Part IV.—
Finance.
34 & 35 Vict.
c. 109.
43 & 36 Vict.
c. 69.

Government Board, and the provisions of the Local Government
(Ireland) Act, 1871, as amended by the Local Government Board
(Ireland) Act, 1872, with respect to the audit of accounts of towns
shall apply as if herein re-enacted, and is terms made applicable to
5 county councils.

(3.) This section shall apply to a county borough.

Local Financial Year and Annual Budget.

39.—(1.) After the appointed day, the local financial year shall
be the twelve months ending the *thirty-first day of March,* and
10 the accounts of the receipts and expenditure of every county council
shall be made up for that year.

(2.) All enactments relating to accounts of local authorities,
or the audit thereof, or to returns touching their receipts and
expenditure, or to meetings, or other matters, shall be modified so
15 far as is necessary for adapting them to this section, and the Local
Government Board shall give such orders and make such arrangements as appear to the Board to be necessary or proper for effecting
such adaptation, and giving effect to this section.

40.—(1.) The expenses incurred by a county and baronial
20 council in the execution of any business transferred or powers and
duties conferred or imposed by this Act, or in discharging their
liabilities, or otherwise under this Act, shall (subject as in this Act
mentioned) be paid out of the county cess.

(2.) At the beginning of every local financial year, every
25 county council shall cause to be submitted to them an estimate of
the receipts and expenses of such council during that year, whether
on account of property, county cess, loans, or otherwise.

(3.) The council shall estimate the amount to be raised in the
first six months, and in the second six months of the financial year,
30 both off the administrative county and off each administrative
barony therein, or any part of such barony.

(4.) If at the expiration of the first six months the council think
that the amount estimated at the beginning of the year will
be larger or smaller than is necessary, they may revise the estimate
35 and alter accordingly the amount of cess.

41.—(1.) The county council having estimated as above provided in this Act the amount to be raised by county cess off each
barony, or part of a barony, during the six months, shall cause
that amount to be applotted by an equal poundage rate upon the
40 property liable in accordance with the enactments relating to the

[174.]   D

appointment of grand jury or county cess, and these enactments shall apply with the substitution of county council for county treasurer.

(2.) Every appointment shall be under the seal of the county council, be publicly notified, and be open for inspection to any cess-payer, and any cess-payer within six weeks after the notification 5 may if he feels aggrieved by such appointment, appeal to sessions in accordance with section twenty-nine of the Local Govern-

ment (Ireland) Act, 1871, and that section shall apply as if the county cess were the rate, and the county council were the governing body therein mentioned, and in this section "cess-payer" 10 shall include any person receiving rent from which any county cess is deducted.

(3.) The estimate shall be prefixed to the appointment and, as well as the demand note, shall be in the prescribed form.

42.—(1.) The expenses of the execution of the business transferred 15 by this Act to county councils from boards of guardians shall be kept separate from the other expenses of the council.

(2.) The former expenses shall be defrayed out of the limited sanitary rate herein-after mentioned; but if in excess of what can be raised by that rate, then out of the ordinary county cess, levied 20 off the district or part of a district liable.

(3.) The limit of the sanitary rate shall be fixed by an order of the Local Government Board which shall be made for each county, as soon as may be, after the passing of this Act, or if respecting business transferred under the Sanitary Acts, after the resolution is 25 confirmed or the Order in Council made by reason of which such transfer takes effect.

(4.) The order shall, in the case of business under the Sanitary Acts, separately limit the rate for general and the rate for special expenses, within the meaning of the Sanitary Acts, and, as regards 30 the latter, separately limit the rate for special expenses in a town as defined by the order and for special expenses elsewhere than in a town so defined.

(5.) The amount to be raised by the sanitary rate shall be estimated and the sanitary rate shall be applotted as part of the county cess, but 35 as a separate item of it, and the sanitary rate shall be for all purposes county cess, save that it shall have the same incidence as the poor rate, and accordingly the occupier of any property may, notwithstanding any provision in this Act, deduct from his rent therefor one half of the amount of the limited sanitary rate applotted on 40 that property, or if the rateable value thereof does not exceed four pounds, the whole of that amount.

(6.) Notice of an order under this section shall be given in the prescribed manner, and if, within three months after such notice, the order is petitioned against by any council, board of guardians, local authority or *twenty* ratepayers affected thereby, it shall, unless
5 the petition is withdrawn, be only a provisional order.

(7.) The amount required to meet the principal and interest of any loans under the Sanitary Acts made before the order shall be raised out of the sanitary rate, notwithstanding it causes an excess above the limit fixed by the order.

10 48.—(1.) Nothing in this Act shall take away any existing power of a judge of assize to make an order which has the force of a presentment, and the county council shall comply with every such order.

(2.) A sum, which is required by law to be raised by way of
15 imperative presentment by the council of any county, or for which a presentment by the grand jury of any county, or an order by a judge of assize in pursuance of the above-mentioned power has been made, shall, as from the time at which it either is so required to be raised or has been presented or ordered, be a debt from the
20 council of that county to the Crown or person to whom that sum is payable, and may be recovered accordingly.

(3.) Where judgment for such debt is recovered, the High Court may appoint a receiver, and confer on such receiver all the power of the county council in relation to receiving,
25 applotting, and levying the county cess; and all officers of the county council, including the baronial constables, shall obey the receiver so empowered; and if any officer fails so to obey the receiver may suspend him and appoint another officer, who shall have the same powers as the suspended officer in respect of the
30 county cess; and the remuneration and expenses of such receiver, to the amount sanctioned by the court, shall be raised by an addition to the county cess levied by the receiver, and be paid thereout, and any surplus of such cess shall be paid to the county treasurer.

(4.) This section shall apply to county boroughs, with the sub-
35 stitution of borough rate for county cess, and any sum required to be raised partly off a county at large and partly off a county borough, shall be apportioned between them in proportion to their rateable value or to the rateable value of those parts of them off which the sum is to be raised.

Part IV.—
Finance.
Supple-
mental pro-
visions as to
Local Taxa-
tion Account.
51 & 52 Vict.
c. 60.

44.—(1.) When a county council, including the council of a county borough, is required under any Act to pay any sum into Her Majesty's Exchequer, or to the Treasury, or to the Board of Works, such sum shall be deducted from the amount payable out of the Local Taxation (Ireland) Account (within the meaning 5 of the Probate Duties (Scotland and Ireland) Act, 1888) to such council, and instead of being paid to the council shall be paid into the Exchequer.

(2.) The account of the receipts and expenditure of the Local Taxation (Ireland) Account shall be audited as a public account 10 by the Comptroller and Auditor-General in accordance with such regulations as the Treasury may make.

(3.) If at any time in any financial year the moneys standing to the Local Taxation (Ireland) Account are insufficient to meet such sums as the Lord Lieutenant considers proper for the time 15 being to pay thereout, the Lord Lieutenant may borrow tem-porarily, and the Bank of Ireland may lend, on the security of the said account, and of moneys becoming payable thereto, the sums he requires for meeting such deficiency, but all sums so borrowed shall be repaid with the interest thereon during the same 20 financial year out of moneys payable to the said account.

Part V.—
Supple-
mental.

Application
of portions
of Municipal
Corporations
(Ireland)
Acts and
other Acts.

PART V.

SUPPLEMENTAL.

Application of Acts.

45. For carrying this Act into effect, the sections of Acts specified 25 in Part One of the Third Schedule to this Act, so far as they are consistent with this Act, and are in force in municipal boroughs, shall apply as if herein re-enacted with the amendments made by this Act and in such terms and with such modifications as are necessary to make them applicable to county and baronial councils, and to 30 their chairman, members, and committees.

Provided as follows:—

(1.) Casual vacancies among the councillors shall be filled by the council.

(2.) The outgoing councillors shall retire on the ordinary day of 35 election of councillors.

(3.) The provisions with respect to the times for holding quarterly meetings shall not apply, but the county council shall hold a quarterly meeting at noon on the *first day of December*, which shall be the ordinary day of election of the chairman of a county council, and such election shall be the first business at the December quarterly meeting.

(4.) The day of the first quarterly meeting of a baronial council in the year beginning with the *twenty-fifth day of November* shall be the ordinary day of election of the chairman of that council.

(5.) The meeting of a county or baronial council, or of any committee thereof, may be held at such place either within or without their county or barony, as the county council direct, and subject to this Act and to the procedure rules may be held on such day as the council think fit.

(6.) Ten days shall be substituted for five days as the time within which a person elected to a corporate office is to accept it, and *twelve months* shall be substituted for six months as the period of absence which disqualifies a councillor.

(7.) Nothing in the said sections shall render a person elected councillor without his previous consent to his nomination liable to pay a fine on non-acceptance of office, or render a chairman or vice-chairman disqualified as such by reason of absence.

46.—(1.) All enactments in any Act, whether general or local, which relate to any business, powers, duties or liabilities transferred by this Act from any authority to a county or baronial council, shall, subject to the provisions of this Act and any procedure rules made thereunder, and so far as circumstances admit, be construed as if—

(a) any reference therein to the said authority or to any committee or member thereof, or to any meeting thereof (so far as it relates to the business, powers, duties, or liabilities transferred) referred to the county or baronial council, or to a committee or member thereof, or to a meeting thereof, as the case requires, and as if—

(b) a reference to the foreman of the grand jury referred to the chairman of the county council; and

(c) a reference to any officer of such authority referred to the corresponding officer of a county council;

and all the said enactments shall be construed with such modifications as may be necessary for carrying this Act into effect.

(2.) Where under the said enactments a person by reason of the office held by him is disqualified for serving on a grand jury, he shall continue to be so disqualified, and shall also be disqualified for serving on the county council.

(3.) Any security required by any of the said enactments shall, 5 instead of being given by recognizance, be given by a covenant under seal with the county council, which may be registered as a recognizance, and when so registered shall be a like charge on the property of the covenantor as if it was a recognizance.

(4.) Where in any of the said enactments anything is to be done 10 on oath or by affidavit, or the grand jury are authorised to administer an oath in relation to any business transferred by this Act to a county council, the same shall be done without an oath or affidavit, or, if so required by the county council, by the production of a statutory declaration, which declaration may be taken before any 15 justice of the peace or commissioner to administer oaths; and the inability of a baronial constable to levy any county cess shall be proved on oath to the satisfaction of two justices.

(5.) For the purposes of this section the expression " authority " means any grand jury, presentment sessions, justices, or boards of 20 guardians, and includes any drainage board, or public body, corporate or unincorporate, specified in a Provisional Order transferring any business to the county council; and the expression " member of an authority " includes, where the authority is a grand jury or justices any grand juror or any justice; and the expression 25 " meeting " in relation to an authority includes assizes and the assembly of a grand jury at assizes and the holding of presentment sessions, and the assembly of justices in petty sessions ; and the expression " clerk of an authority " includes in relation to any grand jury the secretary of the grand jury, and in relation to any 30 justices, the petty sessions clerk.

(6.) This section shall apply to county boroughs.

Incorporation of Councils, their Proceedings and Committees.

47.—(1.) The council of each administrative county shall be a body corporate by the name of the county council with the addition 35 of the name of the county, and shall have perpetual succession and a common seal and power to acquire and hold land for the purposes of their constitution.

(2.) Where any enactment (whether relating to the grand jury or to court or sessions houses or other county purposes,) requires or 40 authorises land to be conveyed or granted to, or any contract or agreement to be made in the name of any commissioners or person

on behalf of the grand jury, or the administrative county, such
land shall be conveyed or granted to, and such contract and
agreement shall be made with, the council of the county concerned.

5 (3.) Any act of a baronial council may be signified in writing
under the hand of any two members of the council countersigned
by the secretary to the county or his deputy.

48.—(1.) The chairman of a county council shall be annually
elected by the council from among the councillors, and shall, by
virtue of his office, be a justice of the peace for the county; but
10 before acting as such justice he shall, if he has not already done
so, take the oaths required by law to be taken by a justice.

(2.) The term of office for the chairman shall be one year, and
he shall continue in office until his successor is appointed, and has
made the required declaration of acceptance of office.

15 (3.) The council may annually appoint a councillor to be vice-
chairman, and, subject to the standing orders of the council, anything authorised or required to be done by, to, or before the
chairman otherwise than as a justice of the peace may be done by,
to, or before such vice-chairman.

20 (4.) The chairman or vice-chairman may resign his office by
writing, under his hand, sent to the vice-chairman or chairman, or
secretary to the county.

(5.) A casual vacancy in the office of chairman or vice-chairman
caused by resignation, death, or disqualification, shall, as soon as
25 practicable be filled up by the council, but the person filling such
vacancy shall retain his office so long only as the vacating
chairman or vice-chairman would have done.

(6.) This section shall apply to baronial councils, except that the
chairman of the baronial council shall not be a justice of the peace.

30 49.—(1.) Every county council shall appoint a finance committee
consisting of not more than one third of their number, for
regulating and controlling the finance of their county; and an
order for paying a sum out of the county fund, whether on account
of capital or income, shall not be made except upon a resolution of
35 the council passed on the recommendation of the finance committee,
and (without prejudice to the provisions of this Act respecting
the standing joint committee) any expense debt or liability
exceeding *fifty pounds* shall not be incurred except upon a resolution of the council passed on an estimate submitted by the finance
40 committee.

(2.) The notice of the meeting of the council at which a resolution for the payment of a sum out of the county fund (otherwise

A.D. 1892.
Part V.—
Supple-
mental.

Election and
position of
chairman and
vice-chair-
man.

Finance
committee.

A.D. 1898.

Part V.—
Supple-
mental.

than for ordinary periodical payments), or a resolution for incurring any expense, debt, or liability exceeding *fifty pounds* will be proposed, shall state the amount of the said sum, expenses, debt, or liability, and the purpose for which it is to be paid or incurred.

Appoint-
ment of
committees
and joint
committees.

50.—(1.) Subject to any regulations made by a council appoint- 5
ing a committee, the proceedings and quorum of the committee, and their place of meeting whether within or without the county, shall be such as the committee direct, and the chairman at any meeting of the committee shall have a second or casting vote. 10

(2.) Any councils may join in appointing out of their respec-
tive bodies a joint committee for the purpose of any business transferred to them by this Act in respect of which they are jointly interested, and each of such councils may delegate to the committee any power of such council for that purpose except 15 the power of raising money by rate or loan.

(3.) Subject to that exception and the terms of delegation, a joint committee shall, as regards any matter delegated to it, have the same power in all respects as the councils appointing it, or any of them, as the case may be, and the provisions of this Act 20 respecting the proceedings and quorum of a committee shall apply to such joint committee, subject to any regulations made jointly by the appointing councils.

(4.) The members of such joint committee shall be appointed at such times and in such manner, and hold office for such period, as 25 may be fixed by the appointing council, if they so long continue without re-election to be members of that council.

(5.) The costs of a joint committee shall be defrayed by the appointing councils in the proportion agreed to by them; and the accounts of such joint committee and their officers shall, for the 30 purposes of this Act, be deemed to be accounts of the respective county councils and their officers.

(6.) This section shall apply to councils of county boroughs.

Supplemen-
tal as to
standing
joint com-
mittee.

51. — (1.) The county council shall annually appoint their repre-
sentatives on the standing joint committee at the meeting for the 35 ordinary election of chairman, and may at any meeting fill up any casual vacancy among their representatives.

(2.) The grand jury shall at the first assizes in every year appoint their representatives on the standing joint committee, each of whom shall own land in the county, either freehold, or 40 leasehold with a term of not less than a *hundred years* unexpired, and of a rateable value not less, if freehold, than *one hundred pounds*, and, if leasehold, than *two hundred pounds*.

A.D. 1891.

Part V.—
Supplemental.

(3.) The grand jury may nominate persons to fill casual vacancies among their representatives, and if at any time, either from want of appointment, or from any casual vacancy, there are not seven representatives of the grand jury on the standing joint committee, 5 the sheriff shall appoint a person in accordance with the said nomination, or if there is no person so nominated who can be appointed, then any properly qualified person to fill the vacancy until the next assizes, and then the grand jury may fill the vacancy.

(4.) Any member of the committee may resign by writing under 10 his hand sent to the chairman of the committee or the secretary to the county.

(5.) The First Schedule shall apply to the proceedings of the committee, and subject thereto the proceedings of the committee shall be regulated by standing orders made by the committee.

15 (6.) The expenses of the standing joint committee shall be defrayed by the county council out of the county rate, as general expenses.

Officers.

52.—(1.) The standing joint committee may appoint and remove the secretary to the county, who shall act as the clerk 20 of the county council and of the standing joint committee, and shall, by himself, or any deputy forming part of the staff of officers hereinafter mentioned, act as the clerk of every baronial council, and perform the duties for the time being required by law to be performed by the secretary of the grand jury, and shall perform 25 such other duties as may be assigned to him by the county council with the concurrence of the standing joint committee.

(2.) The county council shall pay to the secretary to the county such reasonable remuneration as may be fixed by the council, with the concurrence of the standing joint committee, and the 30 remuneration may be in excess of the amount fixed by the Grand Jury Act, 1836, and the Acts amending the same.

(3.) Nothing in this Act shall affect the enactments respecting the appointment of a banking company as treasurer to a county, save that in those enactments the county council shall be sub- 35 stituted for the grand jury.

(4.) Besides such banking company and the secretary to the county, there shall be such staff of officers with such remuneration in each county as may be determined by a scheme of the county council, made with the consent of the Local Government Board, 40 within *six months* after the appointed day, or (if it relates to the officers required for the execution of the Sanitary Acts), after the day on which the transfer of the execution of those Acts to the county council takes effect, or in either case within such further time as may be allowed by the said Board.

(5.) Such scheme may be varied from time to time with the consent of the standing joint committee, or if the county council appeal to the Local Government Board against the refusal of that 5 consent, then with the consent of that Board; save as aforesaid, any increase of the staff or remuneration above that provided by the scheme shall be invalid, but the county council may discontinue or diminish the remuneration of any office of the county except those of the secretary to the county and the county surveyor.   10

(6.) The said staff shall include a county surveyor, and at least one constable in each barony, and for the Sanitary Acts a medical officer of health, and shall include such assistant surveyors, collectors, and other officers and servants, as may be to be necessary or proper for the efficient execution of their business by the 15 county and baronial councils.

(7.) The county council shall appoint a county surveyor, who shall be qualified according to law, but he shall not, unless removed or suspended by the Lord Lieutenant, be dismissed, nor shall his salary be withheld or reduced without the concurrence of the 20 standing joint committee.

(8.) The county council may appoint and remove at their pleasure the other officers, and the power of any officer to appoint any clerk, assistant, or deputy shall cease.

(9.) It shall not be necessary to re-appoint a constable of 25 a barony upon every appointment of county cess, and the security given may be a continuing security so as to extend to all defaults of the constable during his tenure of office.

(10.) The county council shall cause the secretary to the county or other officer to send to the Lord Lieutenant or the Local 30 Government Board such returns and information as may from time to time be required by either House of Parliament.

(11.) No paid officer in the permanent employment of a county council who is required to devote his whole time to such employment shall be eligible to serve in Parliament.   35

(12.) It shall not be lawful to appoint a county councillor or the partner in business of a county councillor to any office or place of profit under the county council or any committee in this Act mentioned; and the disqualification shall apply to any person and his partners in business during *six months* next after such person 40 has ceased to be a county councillor.

(13.) The Local Government Board, on the request of the county council, may hold an inquiry as to the misconduct of any officer and the propriety of removing him, and if the result of the inquiry is adverse to the officer, the consent of the standing joint committee shall not be required for his removal.

(14.) This section shall be without prejudice to the provisions of this Act respecting existing officers.

5

Elections.

53. The election of county and baronial councillors shall, subject to the provisions of this Act, be carried out so far as practicable in the same manner as the election of councillors of a municipal borough, and in the case of a county divided into electoral divisions,
10 of a borough divided into wards; and for that purpose the enactments specified in Part Two of the Third Schedule to this Act so far as they apply to municipal elections in Ireland, shall apply to county and baronial council elections, with the necessary modifications, and in particular with the following additions and
15 modifications :—

(1.) The triennial election of county and baronial councillors shall be conducted together on the *twenty-fifth day of November* in every *third year*, and that day is in this Act referred to as the ordinary day of election of such councillors.

20 (2.) Such person as the county council appoint shall be the returning officer for the election, and without prejudice to any other power, he may by writing under his hand appoint a fit person to be his deputy for all or any of the purposes relating to the election, and may by himself or such deputy exercise any
25 powers and do any things which a returning officer is authorised or required to exercise or do in relation to such election, and shall for the purposes of the election have all the powers of the sheriff at a parliamentary election.

(3.) A reference in this Act, or in the said enactments, to the
30 returning officer or to the mayor or to the alderman shall be construed to refer to the returning officer, and any such deputy as above mentioned.

(4.) A reference in the said enactments to the town clerk shall be construed so far as respects the election to refer to the
35 returning officer or his deputy, and as respects matters subsequent to the election to refer to the county.

(5.) The county court house, or, in an electoral division in which there is no such court house, such sessions court house or other public building as the county council provide, shall be
40 substituted for the town hall.

(6.) The voter may place against the name of any candidate for whom he votes the number of votes he gives to such candidate in

lieu of a cross, and the form of directions for the guidance of
the voter in voting contained in the Ballot Act, 1872, shall be
altered accordingly.

(7.) The returning officer shall forthwith after the election return
the names of the county and baronial councillors to the 5
secretary to the county.

(8.) If a returning officer dies, or is absent, or is otherwise in-
capable of acting, the county council shall forthwith appoint
another person to be returning officer in his place.

(9.) The county council, with the sanction of the Lord 10
Lieutenant, may alter the polling districts and polling places
in their county, but an order so made shall not take effect
until a register of electors can be made to correspond to a
polling district so made, and if made after the *first day of
April* in any year shall not affect the registration during that 15
year. Until any such alteration is made, the polling districts
at the first election shall continue.

(10.) The Municipal Elections (Corrupt and Illegal Practices)
Act, 1884, shall extend to the election of county and baronial
councillors and of councillors and aldermen in county boroughs 20
in like manner as if it were herein re-enacted in such terms
and with such modifications as are necessary to make it applicable to such elections, and in particular with the following :—

(a.) References to Part Four of the Municipal Corporations
Act, 1882, and to the sections therein, shall refer to the 25
Corrupt Practices (Municipal Elections) Act, 1872 and
the corresponding sections therein, and references to other
enactments in force in England shall refer to the corresponding enactments in force in Ireland ;

(b.) The registration rules under this Act shall provide 30
for the proper dealing with the corrupt and illegal
practices list.

54.—(1.) All expenses properly incurred in relation to the
holding of elections of councillors of county and baronial councils
shall be paid out of the county fund as general expenses. 35

(2.) The expenses of any such election shall not exceed those
allowed by the scale framed by the county council with the consent
of the Local Government Board.

(3.) The sections relating to election expenses specified in Part
Three of the Third Schedule to this Act shall apply as if herein re- 40
enacted with the necessary modifications, and in particular with the
substitution of the county council for the person from whom payment
is claimed, and of one month for the period of fourteen days within
which application may be made for taxation.

(4.) A county council shall, on the request of the returning officer, prior to a poll being taken at any election advance to him such sum not exceeding ten pounds for every thousand electors at the election as he may require.

55.—(1.) A person shall be entitled to be registered as a county elector once, but not more than once, in every barony in which he has a qualification, but a person shall not be entitled to vote more than once at the same election of county councillors for a county.

(2.) Subject to registration rules under this section, county electors shall be registered together with and in like manner as parliamentary electors in Ireland.

(3.) Rules (in this Act called registration rules) shall be made by Order in Council for adapting the enactments governing the registration of parliamentary electors in Ireland to the combined registration of parliamentary and county electors, with power to apply any of the enactments governing the combined registration of parliamentary and county electors in England. The registration rules may, with a view to the combined registration determine the forms to be used, and the times and mode at which all matters relating to registration are to be done, and the duties to be performed by clerks of the peace, town clerks, clerks to unions, baronial constables, collectors of poor rates, and other persons, in relation to registration, and may determine the divisions and parts in which, and the manner in which, the lists and registers are to be made out, printed, numbered, and published.

(4.) The revision courts held for revising lists of parliamentary electors shall revise the lists of county electors, with the like powers and duties and subject to the like appeal, and shall be held within the times fixed by the registration rules.

(5.) The register of county electors shall be completed on or before the *seventh day of November* in every year, and shall be the register of county electors for the year beginning that day and ending on the next succeeding *sixth day of November.*

(6.) The provisions of this section shall apply to the enrolment of burgesses in like manner as to the registration of county electors, and the registration rules may assimilate throughout all the county boroughs the duties of town clerks in relation to the combined registration of parliamentary electors and burgesses.

(7.) The registration rules may alter and add to the instructions, precepts, notices, and forms under the enactments relating to the registration of parliamentary electors in Ireland in such manner as appears necessary for carrying into effect this Act and any other Act for the time being in force amending or affecting the said enactments; and the instructions, precepts, notices, and

A.D. 1897.
Part V.—
Supple-
mental.

forms specified in the registration rules shall be observed and be valid in law, and clerks of the peace, town clerks, clerks of the union, and baronial constables and other persons shall act accordingly.

(8.) The expenses of the registration of county electors shall 5 form part of the expenses of the registration of parliamentary electors and be defrayed accordingly, and such expenses shall include any sums payable as herein-after mentioned in respect of the services of the clerk of the peace and baronial constables.

(9.) There may be paid to the clerk of the peace and to baronial 10 constables in a county such remuneration for their duties in relation to the registration of county electors as may be determined by the county council with the consent of the standing joint committee, or in the case of the constables may be fixed by a scheme under this Act, and where the clerk of the peace is in receipt of a salary out 15 of moneys provided by Parliament the said amount shall be added to his salary, and an equal amount shall be paid out of the county cess to the Exchequer.

53 & 54 Vict.
c. 55.

(10.) The scale under the Parliamentary Registration Expenses (Ireland) Act, 1890, for the remuneration of the clerks and col- 20 lectors of poor rates for their services and expenses in carrying into effect the Representation of the People Acts shall include their remuneration for their services and expenses in relation to the registration of county electors under this Act, and any existing scale may be altered so as to give effect to this enactment, and 25 any sum so payable shall be paid out of the poor rate.

Miscellaneous.

Time for
attendance of
grand jury.

56. Notwithstanding anything in section twenty-nine of the Grand Jury Act, 1836, the sheriff shall not be required to summon the grand jury to attend before the day for opening the Commission 30 of Assize, if it appear to him that there is no business which requires their attendance before that day; and any business may without any application to the judge be transacted by the grand jury after the Commission has been opened.

Powers of
Local
Government
Board and
application
of pro-
visions of
41 & 42 Vict.
c. 42.
as to local
inquiries
and pro-
visional
orders.
51 & 52 Vict.
c. 119.

57.—(1.) Where the Local Government Board are required in 35 pursuance of this Act to decide any difference or adjustment or any matter referred to arbitration, the provisions of the Regulation of Railways Act, 1868, respecting arbitrations by the Board of Trade, and the enactments amending those provisions, shall apply as if they were herein re-enacted, and in terms made applicable to the 40 Local Government Board and the decision of differences, adjustments, and matters under this Act.

(2.) Where the Local Government Board are authorised by this Act to make any inquiry, to determine any difference, to

A.D. 1897.

*Part V.—
Supplemental.*

make or confirm any order, or to give any consent, sanction, or
approval to any matter, or otherwise to act under this Act, they
may cause to be made a local inquiry, and in that case, and also in
a case where they are required by this Act to cause to be made a
5 local inquiry, sections two hundred and nine to two hundred and
ten, two hundred and twelve, and two hundred and thirteen of the
Public Health (Ireland) Act, 1878, shall apply as if they were
herein re-enacted, and in terms made applicable to this Act.

(2.) A provisional order under this Act shall be of no effect until
10 it is confirmed by Parliament.

(3.) Sections two hundred and fourteen and two hundred
and fifteen of the Public Health Ireland Act, 1878 (which relate
to the making of provisional orders by the Local Government
Board), shall apply for the purposes of this Act as if herein
15 re-enacted, and in terms made applicable thereto.

(4.) The expenses of any local inquiry held by the Board under
this Act, including a sum on account of the salary of any officer
of the Board engaged therein, shall be paid by the parties to the
inquiry, or by such of them and in such proportions as the Board
20 order, and the amount ordered by the Board to be paid, shall be a
debt to the Crown from the council, authority, or person by whom
it is ordered to be paid.

58.—(1.) The Privy Council on an appeal under this Act may
make such order as to costs, and the parties by whom such costs
25 are to be paid, as they think just.

*Powers of
Privy
Council.*

(2.) All councils, authorities, and persons shall obey any order
made by the Privy Council upon an appeal under this Act, and
every such order shall have effect, and may be enforced, as a
judgment of the High Court.

30 **59.** The Parliamentary Elections Act, 1868, and the Acts
amending the same, shall apply to the trial of a petition for the
removal of councillors as if it were an election petition, subject
to the necessary modifications and in particular as follows :

*Supple-
mental as to
proceedings
before judges
in case of
election
petition.
31 & 32 Vict.
c. 125.*

(a.) The said Act shall apply as if the council charged were the
35 respondent.

(b.) Where the petition alleges any act of a councillor for which
he can be disqualified, that councillor shall be a respondent
to the petition.

(c.) At the conclusion of the trial the judges shall certify their
40 determination and judgment to the Lord Lieutenant, and the
Lord Lieutenant shall thereupon take such proceedings under
this Act as may be necessary.

A.D. 1898.
Part V.—
Supple-
mental.

(d.) The reference to the House of Commons or the Speaker shall not apply.

(e.) It shall not be necessary that any shorthand writer shall attend.

(f.) The rules of court made in pursuance of the said Acts may   5
adapt the same to the trial of a petition under this Act.

Application
to county
of Dublin.

60. In the application of this Act to the county of Dublin, the necessary modifications shall be made, and in particular the following:—

(a.) There shall be substituted—   10

(i.) " A judge of the high court or recorder " for " judge of assize " :

(ii.) " Presenting term " for " assizes " :

(iii.) " District surveyor " for " county surveyor " :

(iv.) " The Grand Jury (Dublin) Act, 1884" for " the Grand   15
Jury Act, 1880."

7 & 8 Vict.
c. 108.

(v.) The sections of the Grand Jury (Dublin) Act, 1844, specified in the first column of the Fourth Schedule to this Act for the sections of the Grand Jury Act, 1836, specified opposite thereto in the second column of that   20
schedule.

(b.) The powers of the finance committee shall be vested in the county council.

(c.) No road wardens shall be appointed, and the duties of road wardens shall be performed by the baronial council :   25

(d.) No district shall be appointed for presentment sessions.

(e.) The High Court shall have no power to fix the place and time of meeting of the council.

Savings.

Saving as to
Parlia-
mentary
elections
and as to
54 & 55 Vict.
c. 48.

61. Nothing in this Act, nor anything done in pursuance of   30
this Act—

(a.) shall alter the limits of any parliamentary borough or parliamentary county, or the right of any person to be registered in any parliamentary register of electors ; or

(b.) shall affect the position of any counties of cities and counties   35
of towns under section twenty-two of the Purchase of Land (Ireland) Act, 1891, or alter the position of any county borough under the said Act, and the provisions of the said sections respecting counties of cities and counties of towns which are considered as included in the counties therein   40
named shall apply to boroughs not heretofore counties of towns which are constituted counties of boroughs by this Act as if they had not been separated from the counties at large.

Definitions.

A.D. 1892.

Part V.—
Supple-
mental.

Interpreta-
tion of
certain terms
in the Act.

45 & 46 Vict.
c. 17.

62. In this Act if not inconsistent with the context, the following terms bare the meanings hereinafter respectively assigned to them ; that is to say :—

5 The expressions "parliamentary county," and "parliamentary election," have the same meaning as in the Parliamentary Registration (Ireland) Act, 1885 :

The expression "parliamentary electors" means persons entitled to vote for a member to serve in Parliament :

10 The expression "occupation electors" means the persons entitled to vote as parliamentary electors in respect of the occupation as owners or tenants of any property :

The expression "barony" includes a half barony :

"The expression "municipal borough" means a municipal 15 borough in which the inhabitants are incorporated, and a council elected under the Municipal Corporations (Ireland) Acts.

The expression "town" includes a township having commissioners :

20 The expression "presentment sessions" means the justices of the peace and associated cesspayers assembled at presentment sessions, either for the barony or for the county at large, as the case requires :

The expression "road authority" means in relation to any town, 25 the commissioners, whether under a general or local Act, having power to maintain and repair the roads in the town :

The expression "Local Government Board" means the Local Government Board for Ireland :

The expression "Board of Works" means the Commissioners of 30 Public Works in Ireland :

The expression "town clerk" means in the case of any town which is not a municipal borough the clerk of the commissioners of that town ;

The expressions "baronial constable" or "constable of a barony" 35 respectively include every collector for a barony or part of a barony, and in case of a collector for part of a barony, the expression "barony" in relation to such collector shall mean that part :

The expression "population" means the population according 40 to the census of one thousand eight hundred and ninety-one :

The expression "road" includes any bridge, pipe, arch, gullet, fence, railing, or wall forming part of such road :

[174]   F

A.D. 1892.

Part V.—
Supplementary.

The expression "rateable value" when used in relation to any
hereditament or area, means the annual rateable value under
the Irish Valuation Acts of such hereditament, or of the
hereditaments comprised in such area :

The expression "prescribed" means prescribed by the Local   5
Government Board :

The expression "existing" means existing at the time specified
in the enactment in which the expression is used, and if no
such time is expressed, then at the day appointed to be for
the purpose of such enactment the appointed day :   10

The expression "property" includes all property, real and personal, and all estates, interests, easements, and rights, whether
equitable or legal, in, to, and out of property real and personal,
including things in action, and registers, books, and documents;
and when used in relation to any grand jury, board of   15
guardians, or other authority, includes any property which on
the appointed day belongs to or is vested in, or held in trust
for, or would but for this Act have, on or after that day,
belonged to, or been vested in, or held in trust for, such grand
jury, board, or other authority :   20

The expression "powers" includes rights, jurisdiction, capacities,
privileges, and immunities :

The expression "duties" includes responsibilities and obligations :

The expression "liabilities" includes liability to any proceeding
for enforcing any duty or for punishing the breach of any   25
duty, and includes all debts and liabilities to which any authority
are or would but for this Act be liable or subject whether
accrued due at the date of the transfer or subsequently accruing,
and includes any obligation to carry or apply any money to
any sinking fund or to any particular purpose.   30

The expression "powers, duties, and liabilities," includes all
powers, duties, and liabilities conferred or imposed by or
arising under any local and personal Act.

Extent of
Act and
short title.

68. This Act shall extend to Ireland only and may be cited as
the Local Government (Ireland) Act, 1892, and the Acts specified 35
in the Second Schedule to the Act are in this Act referred to
collectively and individually by the short titles in that behalf in
that schedule mentioned.

PART VI.
TRANSITORY PROVISIONS.
First Election of County Councillors.

A.D. 1898.

Part VI.—
Transitory
Provisions.

First
election of
county
councillors.

64.—(1.) The first election of county and baronial councillors under this Act shall be held in the month of *January* next after the *passing of this Act*, on such day in each county not earlier than the *fourteenth day of January* as the returning officer for that county may fix, and the returning officer shall publish notice of such day in the preceding month of *December*, and the day so fixed shall be deemed for the purposes of the first election to be the ordinary day of election of county councillors.

(2.) The sheriff of each county shall be the returning officer for such first election, but if the sheriff desires to be a candidate at such election the Local Government Board on his application may appoint another person to be the returning officer, and the person so appointed shall, for the purpose of such election, have the powers and duties of the sheriff.

(3.) For the purpose of the first election every electoral division in a county shall be divided into polling districts by an order of the justices of the county in special sessions confirmed by the Lord Lieutenant and the Privy Council, and for that purpose the Lord Lieutenant shall appoint special general sessions of the justices of the peace to be summoned in every county, and the proceedings shall be taken in accordance with the enactments specified in the Fourth Part of the Third Schedule to this Act and those enactments shall be re-enacted and be deemed to form part of this Act with the modifications made in that schedule.

(4.) At the first election all persons registered in the parliamentary register of electors as occupation electors in respect of property situate in an electoral division or barony, shall be deemed to be duly registered county electors and entitled to vote at the election of councillors for such electoral division or barony; Provided that:—

(a) all persons whose claims are allowed as herein-after mentioned shall also be deemed duly registered county electors and be entitled to vote, and

(b) all persons objections to whose names have been allowed as herein-after mentioned shall, without prejudice to their right to vote at a parliamentary election, be disentitled to vote at the said election of councillors;

and this enactment shall extend to a county borough, with the substitution of burgesses for registered county electors, and of ward for electoral division and the addition of aldermen.

[174.] F 3

A.D. 1892.

*Part VI.—
Transitory
Provisions.*

(5.) Any person entitled, under this Act, to be registered as a county elector or burgess whose name is not entered in the list of parliamentary electors for the current year may claim to have his name entered as a county elector, and any person may object to the name of a person on a list of parliamentary electors on the ground that he is not entitled to be registered as a county elector or burgess.

(6.) The Registration Rules shall provide for such claims and objections being made immediately after the *passing of this Act* within the time and in the manner specified in the Rules, and such claims and objections shall be dealt with by the revision courts in like manner, as near as may be, as claims and objections relating to parliamentary electors.

(7.) The Registration Rules shall provide for the clerk of the peace of every county making making up registers of county and baronial electors so as to serve for the first election of councillors under this Act, and, in the case of a county borough, for such registers being made up before the *eleventh day of November*, and sent to the returning officer of the county borough.

(8.) The returning officer shall send to the secretary to the county the names of the persons elected, and shall send to each person elected a county or baronial councillor notice of his election, accompanied in the case of a county councillor by a summons to attend the first meeting of the provisional council fixed by this Act at such time and place as the returning officer may fix.

(9.) The costs properly incurred by the returning officer in reference to the first election and in reference to the first meeting of the provisional council, shall be defrayed as expenses of the county council, and may be taxed on an application made by or by direction of the provisional council.

Retirement
of first
county
councillors.

65.—The county and baronial councillors elected at the first election shall retire from office on the ordinary day of election in the *third calendar year after the passing of this Act*, and their places shall be filled by a new election.

Addition of
ex officio
councillors
to each
council.

66.—In addition to the elected councillors, the following persons shall be councillors of the first county council in like manner as if elected at the first election under this Act, that is to say, the persons who at the date of such first election are lieutenant of the county and high sheriff of the county, one person nominated by the grand jury at the first assizes held next after the *passing of this Act*, and one person nominated before the appointed day by the presentment sessions for the county at large.

(3.) In addition to the baronial councillors elected under this Act, one person nominated before the appointed day by the presentment sessions of the barony, shall be a councillor of the first council of the barony in like manner as if elected councillor at the first 5 election under this Act.

(4.) The additional councillors under this section shall be subject to removal as elected councillors and shall cease to hold office on the first retirement of councillors under this Act.

67.—(1.) The councillors of the first county or baronial council 10 shall not enter on their ordinary duties or become the council until the *first day of April* next after their election, or such other day as, on the application of the provisional council, the Local Government Board may appoint.

(2.) The councillors of a county council shall, on the second 15 Thursday next after the day of the first election, and thenceforward until the day above mentioned in this section, meet and act as a provisional council for arranging to bring this Act into operation.

(3.) The provisional council shall, at their first meeting, or some 20 adjournment thereof, elect one of their number to be chairman, and may fill any vacancy in the office of such chairman, and the person elected chairman shall be chairman of the provisional council, and also on and after the appointed day of the county council, and the term of office of such chairman shall end on the next ordinary 25 day of election of chairman; and this enactment shall extend to the vice-chairman.

(4.) The provisional council, after disposing of the preliminary business, shall proceed to provide for bringing the various provisions of this Act into full operation on the appointed day or days, 30 and to frame a scheme for the officers, and to provide for all matters which appear necessary or proper for enabling the county and baronial councils as constituted under this Act to execute their duties, and for giving full effect to this Act.

(5.) The enactments respecting the proceedings of the county 35 council, shall apply to the proceedings of the provisional council, and any act of the provisional council may be signified under the hand of the chairman and any two members of the council countersigned by the officer acting as their secretary.

(6.) The provisional council of a county shall be entitled to use 40 the county court house, so that they do not interfere with the holding of any court, and the secretary of the grand jury shall, if required, act as the secretary of the provisional council and

A.D. 1892.
Part VI.—
Transitory
Provisions.

the provisional council may hire such buildings and appoint such interim officers as appear to them necessary for the performance of their duties, and the expenses of so doing or otherwise of the performance of their duties shall be defrayed as expenses properly incurred by the county council.   5

(7.) There shall be paid out of the county cess to the secretary of the grand jury such reasonable remuneration as the grand jury award for extra services rendered by him in bringing this Act into operation, and in acting as secretary of the provisional council and secretary to the county until his salary is fixed.   10

(8.) The provisional council shall have the same power of levying county cess for the purpose of their costs and for the future costs of the county council as if they were constituted a county council.

(9.) The presentment sessions for every county at large, and every board of guardians in a county, shall, by the appointment of 15 committees, or the holding of sessions and meetings, and otherwise, make such provisions as are necessary or proper for making arrangements with the provisional council for carrying this Act into effect; and the sessions may meet for that purpose on such days and at such times and places as they think fit to appoint, and 20 the secretary of the grand jury shall summon the first meeting for the purpose to meet at the county court house on some convenient day in *January* next after the *passing of this Act*.

General Provision as to First Elections.

Casual
vacancies
at first
elections,
and first
meetings.

68.—(1.) If at the first election a person is elected a county 25 councillor for more than one electoral division of the same county his choice as to the division for which he will serve shall be made by writing addressed to the returning officer, and the returning officer, if he has not received the above before the first meeting of the provisional council, shall determine the division for which such 30 person shall serve.

(2.) A casual vacancy arising at the first election from a person being elected for more than one electoral division, or from a failure of election or otherwise, may be filled by the provisional council.

(3.) Such councillors as have been elected for a county council 35 at the first election shall, subject to any order of the Local Government Board to the contrary under this Act, proceed to act as a provisional council under this Act, notwithstanding any vacancy or vacancies arising from failure of election or otherwise.

A.D. 1898.

Part VI.—
Transitory
Provisions.

(4.) In case of equality of votes at the first meeting of a provisional county council, the chairman of the meeting shall have a second or casting vote, and where on the selection of the chairman of the first meeting an equal number of votes is given to
5 two or more persons, the meeting shall determine by lot which of those persons shall be the chairman.

(5.) The first meeting of the council shall be held on the day appointed for the council coming into office, and shall be convened by the chairman of the provisional county council.

10 (6.) Such first meeting, and also the first meeting of the provisional county council, shall be convened in like manner as meetings of the county council, and as if the person convening the same were the chairman.

(7.) This section shall apply to a baronial council with the
15 substitution of barony for county, except that there shall be no provisional council, and the first meeting shall be convened by the chairman of the provisional county council.

Power of
Local
Government
Board to
remedy
defects.

69.—(1.) If from any cause there is no returning officer able to act in any county at the first election of a county council, or no register
20 of electors properly made up, or no proper election takes place, or an election of an insufficient number of persons takes place, or any difficulty arises as respects the holding of the first election of county councillors, or as to the first meeting of a provisional council or baronial council, the Local Government Board may by order
25 appoint a returning officer or other officer, and do any matter or thing which appears to them necessary for the proper holding of the first election, and for the proper holding of the first meeting of the provisional council and baronial council, and may, if it appears to them necessary, direct a new election to be held, and fix the
30 dates requisite for such new election. Any such order may modify the provisions of this Act and the enactments applied by this Act so far as may appear to the Board necessary for the proper holding of the first election and first meeting of the provisional council and baronial council.

35 (2.) The Local Government Board, on the application of a county or baronial council or of a provisional council, may, within six months after the day fixed for the first election of the councillors of such council, make such orders as appear to them necessary for bringing this Act into full operation as respects the
40 council so applying, and such orders may modify any enactment in

A.D. 1895.

Part VI.—
Transitory
Provisions.

Appointed
day.

Current
rates, legal
proceedings,
&c.

this or any other Act, whether general or local and personal, so far as may appear to the Board necessary for the said purpose.

(3.) This section shall apply to county boroughs.

Appointed Day.

70.—(1.) Subject as in this Act mentioned, the appointed day 5 for the purposes of this Act shall in each county be the *first day of April* next after the *passing* of this Act, or as respects business under the Sanitary Act after the transfer of the business, or in any case such other day, earlier or later, as the Local Government Board (but after the election of 10 county councillors for a county on the application of the provisional council or county council) may appoint, either generally or with reference to any particular provision of this Act, and different days may be appointed for different purposes and different provisions of this Act, whether contained in the same 15 section or in different sections or for different counties.

(2.) Save so far as there may be anything in the context inconsistent therewith, any enactment of this Act shall come into operation on the appointed day.

(3.) This section shall apply to county boroughs. 20

Transitional Proceedings.

71.—(1.) Every cess and rate made before the appointed day may be levied, and proceedings for the enforcement thereof taken in like manner as if this Act had not passed.

(2.) The accounts of all receipts and expenditure before the ap- 25 pointed day shall be audited, and disallowances, surcharges, and penalties recovered and enforced, and other consequential proceedings had in like manner as if this Act had not passed, and every officer whose duty it is to make up any accounts, or to account for any portion of the receipts or expenditure in any 30 account, shall, until the audit is completed, be deemed for the purpose of such audit to continue in office and be bound to perform the same duties and render the same accounts, and be subject to the same liabilities as before the appointed day.

(3.) All proceedings, legal and other, commenced before the 35 appointed day, may be carried on in like manner as if this Act had not passed, and may be so carried on by the county council in substitution for the authorities by whom such proceedings were commenced. Every legal proceeding commenced before the appointed day may be amended in such manner as may appear necessary or 40 proper in order to bring the same into conformity with this Act.

72. At the expiration of *three months* after the appointed day, the existing governors and directors of every district lunatic asylum shall cease to hold office unless re-appointed by the Lord Lieutenant.

Existing Officers.

73.—(1.) The existing secretary to the grand jury in each county shall be the first secretary to that county under this Act.

(2.) The existing county surveyor in each county shall continue to be surveyor of that county.

(3.) The existing treasurer in each county shall continue to be treasurer of that county, and where such treasurer is not a banking company, he shall hold office by the same tenure as is fixed by this Act for the county surveyor.

(4.) All other existing officers appointed by the grand jury of a county, or appointed by any such officer under a statutory power and paid out of the county cess shall continue in office as officers of the council of the county, and all persons appointed baronial constables in a county at the assizes next before the *passing of this Act*, shall continue in office as existing officers of the council of such county.

(5.) All the existing officers above mentioned shall hold office by the tenure and on the terms and conditions fixed by this Act for the like officers, and while performing their duties shall receive not less salaries and remuneration and be entitled to not less pensions (if any) than if this Act had not passed. Provided that if any existing officer who holds office at the pleasure of the county council is removed or has his remuneration reduced or suspended, without such cause as in the case of an appeal by the officer to the standing joint committee appears to the standing joint committee to be sufficient, that officer shall be entitled to compensation.

(6.) The scheme mentioned in this Act relating to the staff of officers may distribute the business to be performed by existing officers in such manner as may be considered just, and every existing officer shall perform such duties in relation to that business as may be directed by the scheme, and shall not, except with the concurrence of the standing joint committee, be called upon to perform any other duties.

(7.) The said scheme or the county council may abolish the office of any existing officer whose office they may deem unnecessary, but such officer shall be entitled to compensation under this Act.

(8.) The county surveyor and the officers appointed by him or by the grand jury of a county of a city or town shall become officers of the council of such county of a city or town in like manner as if they had been appointed under the Municipal Corporations (Ireland) Acts.

A.D. 1892.

Part VI.—
Transitory Provisions.
As regarding of existing governors and directors of lunatic asylums.

As to officers transferred to county councils.

A.D. 1892.
Part VI.—
Treasury
Provisions.
Compensation to existing officers.

74.—(1.) Every existing officer declared by this Act to be entitled to compensation, and every other existing officer, whether before mentioned in this Act or not, who by virtue of this Act, or anything done in pursuance of or in consequence of this Act, suffers any direct pecuniary loss by abolition of office or by 5 diminution or loss of fees or salary, shall be entitled to compensation for such pecuniary loss from the county council, to whom the business of the authority, whose officer he was, is transferred under this Act, regard being had to the conditions on which his appointment was made, to the nature of his office or employment, 10 to the duration of his service, to any additional emoluments which he acquires by virtue of this Act, or of anything done in pursuance of or in consequence of this Act, and to all the other circumstances of the case, and the compensation shall not exceed the amount which, under the Acts and rules relating to 15 Her Majesty's Civil Service, is paid to a person on abolition of office.

3 & 4 Will. 4.
c. 84.

(2.) Every person entitled to compensation as above mentioned, shall deliver to the county council a claim under his hand setting forth the whole amount received and expended by him or his prede- 20 cessors in office, in every year during *five years* next before the *passing of this Act*, on account of the emoluments for which he claims compensation, distinguishing the offices in respect of which the emoluments were received, and accompanied by a statutory declaration that the statement is true according to the best of his 25 knowledge, information, and belief.

(3.) Such statement shall be submitted to the county council, who shall forthwith take the same into consideration, assess the just amount of compensation (if any), and inform the claimant of their decision. 30

(4.) If a claimant is aggrieved by the refusal of the county council to grant any compensation, or by the amount of compensation assessed, or if not less than one third of the councillors of such council subscribe a protest against the amount of the compensation as being excessive, the claimant or any subscriber to 35 such protest (as the case may be) may, within three months after the decision of the council, appeal to the Treasury, who shall consider the case and determine whether any compensation, and if so, what amount ought to be granted to the claimant, and such determination shall be final. 40

(5.) Any claimant under this section, if so required by any county councillor, shall attend at a meeting of the council and answer all questions asked by any councillor touching the matters

A. D. 1892.

*Part VI.—
Treasury
Provisions.*

set forth in his claim, and shall further produce all books, papers, and documents in his possession or under his control relating to such claim, and if so required shall verify the answers to such questions and the production of the books, paper, and documents,
5 by a statutory declaration.

(6.) The compensation payable in pursuance of this section shall begin at the date fixed by the council on granting it, or, in case of appeal, by the Treasury, and shall be a specially debt due to the person entitled from the county council.

10 (7.) If a person receiving compensation in pursuance of this section is appointed to any office under the same or any other county council, or by virtue of this Act, or anything done in pursuance of or in consequence of this Act, receives any increase of emoluments of the office held by him, he shall not, while receiving the
15 emoluments of that office, receive any greater amount of his compensation, if any, than, with the emoluments of the said office, is equal to the emoluments for which compensation was granted to him, and if the emoluments of the office he holds are equal to or greater than the emoluments for which compensation was granted,
20 his compensation shall be suspended while he holds such office.

(8.) All expenses incurred by a county council under this section shall be paid out of the county fund as general expenses.

Savings.

*Saving for
existing
securities
and dis-
charge of
debts.*

75.—(1.) Nothing in this Act shall prejudicially affect any
25 securities granted before the *passing of this Act* on the credit of any cess or rate or of any property by this Act transferred to a county council; and all such securities, as well as all unsecured debts incurred by any authority in the exercise of any powers, or in relation to any property, transferred to the county council shall
30 be discharged, paid, and satisfied by such council.

(2.) Where for the purpose of satisfying any such security or any debt, it is necessary to continue the levy of any rate or cess or the exercise of any power which would have existed but for the provisions of this Act, such rate or cess may continue to be
35 levied and power to be exercised either by the authority who otherwise would have levied or exercised the same or by the county council, as the case may require.

(3.) It shall be the duty of every authority whose business is transferred to any council by this Act to liquidate so far as prac-
40 ticable before the date of such transfer all current debts incurred by such authority so far as relates to the business so transferred.

A.D. 1892.

Part VI.—
Treasury
Provisions.

Saving for
pending
actions, con-
tracts, &c.

76.—(1.) If at the date of the transfer of any business powers, duties, liabilities, or property to a county or baronial council, any action or proceeding, or any cause of action or proceeding in relation thereto is pending or existing by or against any authority the same shall not be in anywise prejudicially affected by the 5 passing of this Act, but may be continued, prosecuted, and enforced by or against such council as successors of the said authority in like manner as if this Act had not passed.

(2.) All contracts, deeds, bonds, agreements, and other instruments entered into or made by any authority and subsisting at the time 10 of the transfer in this section mentioned, and affecting the subject-matter of the transfer, shall be of as full force and effect against or in favour of the council, and may be enforced as fully and effectually, as if, instead of the authority, the said council had been a party thereto. 15

(3.) This section shall apply in the case of a committee of any authority in like manner as if the committee were such authority, and the committee of a county council were that council.

Saving for
charters,
local Acts,
&c.

77. Save so far as may be necessary to give effect to this Act or any order or other thing made or done thereunder nothing 20 in this Act shall prejudicially alter or affect the powers, rights, privileges, or immunities of any municipal corporation, or the operation of any municipal charter, local Act of Parliament, or order confirmed by Parliament, which immediately before the passing of this Act was in force. 25

Repeals.

Repeal of
Acts.

78. All enactments inconsistent with this Act are hereby repealed: Provided that any enactment or document referring to any Act or enactment hereby repealed shall be construed to refer to this Act, or to the corresponding enactment in this Act. 80

SCHEDULES.

FIRST SCHEDULE.

Proceedings of Standing Joint Committee.

(1.) The committee shall annually elect one of their own number to be chairman, and in the event of an equality of votes at the election of chairman, the matter shall be decided by lot.

(2.) The quorum of the committee shall be six.

(3.) The secretary to the county shall summon meetings of the committee at the times required by any standing orders, and at any time on the requisition of the chairman, or of any two members of the committee.

(4.) A meeting shall be summoned by notice sent to each member of the committee not less than six days previously, specifying the matters to be transacted at the meeting.

(5.) Subject to the foregoing provisions the proceedings of the committee shall be regulated by standing orders made by the committee.

(6.) The committee may act notwithstanding any vacancy in their number.

SECOND SCHEDULE.

ACTS REFERRED TO.

PART I.

Acts referred to.	Title.	Short Title.
6 & 7 Will. 4. c. 116.	An Act to consolidate and amend the laws relating to the presentment of public money by grand juries in Ireland.	The Grand Jury Act, 1836.
7 & 8 Vict. c. 106.	An Act to consolidate and amend the laws for the regulation of grand jury presentments in the county of Dublin.	The Grand Jury (Dublin) Act, 1844.
30 & 31 Vict. c. 112.	An Act to provide further facilities for the repair of roads, bridges, and other public works in Ireland in case of sudden damage.	The Roads Act, 1867.

PART II.

The Acts in this Part are referred to as the Municipal
Corporations (Ireland) Acts.

Acts referred to.	Title.	Short Title.
3 & 4 Vict. c. 108.	An Act for the regulation of Municipal Corporations in Ireland.	The Municipal Corporations (Ireland) Act, 1840.
5 & 6 Vict. c. 104.	An Act to explain and amend certain enactments contained respectively in the Acts for the regulation of Municipal Corporations in England and Wales and in Ireland.	The Municipal Corporations Act, 1842.
6 & 7 Vict. c. 93.	An Act to amend an Act of the the third and fourth years of Her present Majesty for the regulation of municipal corporations in Ireland.	The Municipal Corporations (Ireland) Act, 1843.
15 & 16 Vict. c. 5.	An Act further to explain and amend the Acts for the regulation of municipal corporations in England, Wales, and Ireland.	The Municipal Corporations Act, 1852.
22 Vict. c. 35.	The Municipal Corporation Act, 1859.	
23 & 24 Vict. c. 16.	The Municipal Corporation Mortgages, &c., Act, 1860.	
23 & 24 Vict. c. 71.	An Act to amend the provisions of the Act for the regulation of municipal corporations in Ireland with respect to the appointment of coroners in boroughs.	The Borough Coroners (Ireland) Act, 1860.
31 & 32 Vict. c. 26.	An Act to make provision for the payment of salaries to clerks of the peace and clerks of the Crown in certain boroughs in Ireland.	The Borough Clerks of the Peace Act, 1868.
38 & 39 Vict. c. 40.	The Municipal Elections Act, 1875.	
39 & 40 Vict. c. 76.	The Municipal Privilege Act, Ireland, 1876.	
41 & 42 Vict. c. 51.	The Municipal Elections (Ireland) Act, 1878.	
48 & 49 Vict. c. 9.	The Municipal Voters Relief Act, 1885.	
51 & 52 Vict. c. 34.	The Municipal Local Bills (Ireland) Act, 1888.	
51 & 52 Vict. c. 53.	The Borough Funds (Ireland) Act, 1888.	

THIRD SCHEDULE.

ENACTMENTS APPLIED.

PART I.

Municipal Corporations.

Municipal Corporations (Ireland) Act, 1840. 3 & 4 Vict. c. 108.	Section fifty-eight, section sixty-three, section eighty-five, section eighty-six, section eighty-seven, section eighty-eight, section eighty-nine, section ninety-two, section ninety-five, section one hundred and two, section one hundred and twenty-five to one hundred and twenty-seven, section one hundred and thirty-seven, and section one hundred and thirty-nine.
The Municipal Corporations Act, 1861. 5 & 6 Vict. c. 104.	Section seven and section eight.
The Municipal Corporations (Ireland) Act, 1843. 6 & 7 Vict. c. 93.	Section eight.
The Municipal Corporations Act, 1855. 18 & 19 Vict. c. 5.	Section two and section six.
The Municipal Corporation Mortgages, &c. Act, 1860. 23 & 24 Vict. c. 16.	Section one to five, and section seven to nine.
The Debtors Act (Ireland), 1872. 35 & 36 Vict. c. 57.	Section twenty.
The Municipal Privilege Act, Ireland, 1876. 39 & 40 Vict. c. 76.	Section ten.
The Public Health (Ireland) Act, 1878. 41 & 42 Vict. c. 52.	Section two hundred and twenty-four.
The Town Councils and Local Boards Act, 1880. 43 Vict. c. 17.	Section one.

Part II.
Elections.

The Municipal Corporations (Ireland) Act, 1840. 3 & 4 Vict. c. 108.	Section sixty-three, section sixty-five, section sixty-six, section sixty-seven, section sixty-eight, section sixty-nine, section seventy-four.	5
The Municipal Corporation Act, 1859. 22 Vict. c. 35.	Section eight.	
The Local Government (Ireland) Act, 1871. 34 & 35 Vict. c. 109.	Sections twenty, twenty-one.	10
The Ballot Act, 1872. 35 & 36 Vict. c. 33.	The whole Act so far as relates to municipal elections in Ireland.	
The Corrupt Practices (Municipal Elections) Act, 1872. 35 & 36 Vict. c. 60.	The whole Act so far as it relates to municipal elections in Ireland.	15
The Municipal Elections Act, 1875. 38 & 39 Vict. c. 40.	The whole Act, so far as it relates to municipal elections in Ireland, except sections six, nine, and ten.	20
The Municipal Elections (Ireland) Act, 1879. 42 & 43 Vict. c. 33.	Section 2 except provisos (2) to (5).	
The Election (Hours of Poll) Act, 1885. 48 & 49 Vict. c. 10.	The whole Act so far as it relates to municipal elections in Ireland.	25

Part III.
Election Expenses.

The Parliamentary Elections (Returning Officers) Act, 1875. 38 & 39 Vict. c. 84.	Section four, section five, section seven, and Second Schedule.	30
The Parliamentary Elections (Returning Officers) Act, 1875, Amendment Act, 1886. 49 & 50 Vict. c. 37.	Section one.	35

PART IV.

Enactments relative to new polling districts and polling places.

A.D. 1898.

Section and Chapter.	Title.	Enactments applied.
35 & 36 Vict. c. 33	The Ballot Act, 1872	Section eighteen, sub-sections one to seven, both included; sub-section seventeen, sub-section nineteen.
36 & 37 Vict. c. 8.	The Polling Districts (Ireland) Act, 1873.	Section one.

Modifications to be made in the above enactments for the purposes of this Act.

(i.) In sub-section (1) the first day of September shall be substituted for the first day of November, and the purpose for which the special sessions shall be appointed shall be for dividing electoral divisions into polling districts and appointing polling places for such districts.

(ii.) In sub-section (4) the first day of October shall be substituted for the first day of December; and the words "electoral divisions" shall be substituted for county or riding where those words secondly occur; and the words "county councillors" shall be substituted for the words "members to serve in Parliament."

(iii.) Any reference to "this Act" contained in the above enactments of the Ballot Act, 1872, shall be construed to refer to this Act and not to the Ballot Act, 1872.

(iv.) In sub-section one of section one of the Polling Districts (Ireland) Act, 1873, the expression "said orders made before the passing of this Act" shall be construed to refer to orders under this Act.

FOURTH SCHEDULE.

Corresponding Sections of Grand Jury Act, 1836, and Grand Jury (Dublin) Act, 1844.

The following Sections of Grand Jury (Dublin) Act, 1844.	Sections of Grand Jury Act, 1836, for which they are to be substituted.
Section eighty.	Section eighteen.
Section one hundred and nine.	Section forty-nine.
Section forty-one.	Section one hundred and six.
Section one hundred and twenty-two.	Section one hundred and thirty-five.

Local Government (Ireland).

A

B I L L

For amending the Law relating to Local
Government in Ireland, and for other
purposes connected therewith.

*(Prepared and brought in by
Mr. Balfour, Mr. Jackson, Mr. Ritchie, and
Mr. Attorney-General for Ireland.)*

Ordered, by The House of Commons, to be Printed,
18 February 1892.

PRINTED BY EYRE AND SPOTTISWOODE,
PRINTERS TO THE QUEEN'S MOST EXCELLENT MAJESTY.

And to be purchased, either directly or through any Bookseller, from
EYRE and SPOTTISWOODE, East Harding Street, Fleet Street, E.C.,
and 32, Abingdon Street, Westminster, S.W.; or
JOHN MENZIES & Co., 12, Hanover Street, Edinburgh, and
90, West Nile Street, Glasgow; or
HODGES, FIGGIS, & Co., 104, Grafton Street, Dublin.

(*Price 6d.*)

[Bill 174.]